Party and Participation in British Elections

Party and Participation in British Elections

by
Anthony Mughan

 Frances Pinter (Publishers) London

First published in Great Britain in 1986 by
Frances Pinter (Publishers) Ltd
25 Floral Street, London WC2E 9DS

British Library Cataloguing in Publication Data

Mughan, A.
 Party and Participation in British
 Elections.
 1. Great Britain. *Parliament. House of
 Commons* — Elections — History 2. Voting
 — Great Britain — History — 20th century
 I. Title
 324.941'0858   JN956

ISBN 0-86189-608-3

Typeset in Australia
Printed by Biddles of Guildford

Contents

Acknowledgements   vii

**1 The underdeveloped study of voting
   turnout**   1

   Introduction   1
   The voting act   4
   Research design   7
     Research objectives   7
     Design problems   13
   Format of presentation   16

**2 The pattern and long-term determinants
   of turnout**   22

   The institutional framework   22
   Patterns of turnout   26
   Long-term determinants of turnout   30

3 The political context and turnout   41

   Introduction   41
   The political context   42
   Level of turnout   49
   Rate of change of turnout   61
   Conclusion   68

**4 The candidates in the constituency
   and turnout**   75

   Introduction   75
   Candidate characteristics   76
   Level of turnout   82
   Rate of change of turnout   97
   Conclusion   102

Contents

**5 The national standing of the parties
and turnout**   111

Introduction   111
National standing of the parties   113
Level of turnout   116
Rate of change of turnout   127
Conclusion   134

6 Conclusion   142

Appendix   154

Index   158

Acknowledgements

The research for this book was carried out with the assistance of grants from the Nuffield Foundation Small Grants Scheme and the Economic and Social Research Council. The Australian National University and University College, Cardiff were unstintingly generous in their provision of computing and secretarial facilites. Christine Treadwell of The Australian National University is responsible for much of the typing and worked patiently and skilfully to get the manuscript into final shape. The election data come from the useful publications of F.W.S. Craig and much of it was collected by Martin Shepherd, who first stimulated my interest in by-elections. A number of people, including John Cross, Martin Harrop, Ian McAllister and Vance Merrill, made valuable comments on earlier drafts of the individual chapters and I would like to thank them. My special thanks in this regard go to Clive Bean for his careful and incisive reading of the final manuscript. Lastly, I would like to acknowledge the more indirect contributions of Robert McKinlay, for his intellectual stimulation, and of Karen and Siân, who suffer through my academic efforts with tolerance and understanding.

1   The Underdeveloped Study of Voting Turnout

Introduction

The cardinal principle of liberal democracy is the primacy of the citizen over the state and the institutional means of putting this principle into practice is the participation of the mass public in the governmental decision-making process. In an ideal world, this participation would be direct and continuous, as, for example, in the fabled New England town meeting. If only for the logistical problems raised by the physical size of modern states, however, direct democracy of this type has never been feasible. Instead, other institutional arrangements have evolved to seek to ensure that governments remain responsive to the will of the people and that the overriding goal of popular control of government be attained. Apart from the relatively rare phenomenon of direct consultation through plebiscites and referendums, these arrangements enshrine the institution of indirect citizen participation. The citizenry as a whole may not be directly involved in the making of governmental decisions, but in theory it can influence these decisions by way of its right, firstly, to choose its governors through periodic elections and, secondly, to organise itself politically to influence the authoritative, day-to-day decisions of those so elected. Political participation is thus commonly defined as those 'legal activities by private citizens which are more or less directly aimed at influencing the selection of governmental personnel and or the actions they take'.[1]

The activities falling under the umbrella of political participation are manifold. At one extreme is to be found relatively simple and effortless acts like initiating political discussion and turning out to vote, whereas at the other is to be found far more demanding and time-consuming undertakings like holding office in a local party organisation or standing for elective office. Between these two extremes, there is a large number of more sporadic forms of intense political involvement, usually crystallising at election time. These include contacting elected representatives, attending political meetings and constituency campaign activity in the form of canvassing, displaying and distributing party propaganda, raising and contributing funds, and so on.[2]

This book is concerned with only one of these various forms of political involvement, electoral participation (or voting turnout). Its importance is not that it is necessarily among the more influential participatory acts. Indeed, there is a large 'rational choice' literature questioning whether it is sensible to bother voting at all since the likelihood of an individual's vote determining the outcome of an election, even in a single constituency never mind the nation as a whole, is virtually nil.[3] Instead, voting's importance is more symbolic; being the single participatory act in which most people engage, it comes to be synonymous with democracy itself. Even in a country where turnout at the polls is as notoriously low as the United States, '(v)oting is the political act in which more citizens engage than any other. In the presidential elections between 1952 and 1976, actual turnout averaged 61.4 per cent. No other political act came even close to that level of citizen participation; the nearest rival, reported attempts to persuade others how to vote, averaged only 31.7 per cent'.[4] Not surprisingly, therefore, open elections are commonly held to be the defining characteristic of liberal democracy. 'Democracy exists where the principal leaders of a political system are selected by competitive elections in which the bulk of the population have the opportunity to participate.'[5]

The right to participate in 'free and competitive' elections being the cornerstone of democracy, it is small wonder that a vast literature has arisen on the determinants of electoral participation. Oversimplifying drastically, this literature can be grouped into three categories, which can be labelled 'sociological', 'attitudinal' and 'political' respectively. The sociological literature emphasises the social and economic characteristics differentiating voters and non-voters. It has been repeatedly established, for example, that the higher an individual's socioeconomic status, the more likely that person is to vote.[6] In the specific context of the United States, recent research points more discriminatingly to 'the transcendent importance of education...(T)he personal qualities that raise the probability of voting are the skills that make learning about politics easier and more gratifying and reduce the difficulties of voting'.[7] More generally, what applies to individuals also applies to political systems as a whole; the more socioeconomically developed is a country, the higher will be the level of voting turnout in it.[8]

The attitudinal literature, in contrast, sees pyschological variables as providing the decisive stimulus to participation, its basic point being that socioeconomic stimuli are filtered through the individual pysche. Attitudes may be socioeconomically determined to some extent, but this dependence is not deemed to detract from their predictive or explanatory preeminence. Works emphasising attitudes as independent influences on participation look at the effects of such psychological variables as a sense of political efficacy, citizen duty, political interest and concern, and identification with a political party.[9] This range of attitudes is widened in political culture studies of participation to encompass others like a a feeling of pride in one's political system and an appreciation of the relevance of government.[10]

The political literature concentrates less on the participants themselves and more on the wide range of exogenous factors mediating their involvement in the electoral process. One set of such factors bears on the growth of party organisation at the local level with the spread of the franchise and its effect on turnout patterns in the electorate.[11] Another set of political determinants involves the legal and administrative arrangements governing the conduct of elections. Relevant considerations here range from the type of electoral system to provisions for absentee voting, usually through some variant of the postal vote.[12] Such provisions generally serve to encourage voting. Others, however, can discourage it, even if inadvertently. Registration laws and residency requirements often fall into this latter category; even the most aggressive participant cannot hope to vote if he fails to satisfy one or other of these requirements. A recent study of the United States, for example, concludes: 'If every state had registration laws in 1972 as permissive as those in the most permissive states, turnout would have been about 9 percentage points higher in the presidential election.'[13]

This brief overview, then, highlights the differences in explanatory perspective and emphasis between the three groups of turnout studies. But their differences notwithstanding, these studies also have much in common. In particular, they are concerned almost exclusively to explain long-term stability in patterns of voting turnout with the result that the explanation of short-term variation in these patterns across electoral units is neglected. That is, they are preoccupied with explanatory variables that crucially underpin the 'normal' participatory configuration of societies and whose effect is unlikely to change appreciably even over the medium term, never mind from one election to the next. Moreover, if their effect does change, it is lasting and the parameters of the participatory configuration of society are redefined. For instance, the 1924 legislation introducing compulsory voting into Australian federal elections moved the level of institutionalised voting turnout onto a higher plane, whereas its removal from Dutch elections in 1970 had precisely the opposite effect.[14]

The Voting Act

Requiring the least initiative and effort, the voting act is the most common mode of political participation. It is also an act that consists of two closely related dimensions, the casting of the ballot to which one is entitled and the choice of a candidate or party for which to vote. The two dimensions are not mutually exclusive, however. In sequential terms, electors must go to the polls before they can make their voting choice known, but it is also the case that if this choice has not been made beforehand, then voters are less likely to show up at the polls in the first place. Turnout and choice, in other words, stand in a symbiotic relationship to each other. Yet, there is a severe imbalance in our understanding of each of them separately and, hence, of the voting act as a whole. The essence of this imbalance is that we understand the short-term dynamics of voting choice far better than the short-term dynamics of voting turnout.

Perusing the voting turnout literature, one is forcefully struck by its continued intellectual resemblance to the early voting choice studies. These were conducted by American sociologists in the late 1940s, which was an era of electoral hegemony for the Democratic party insofar as it had monopolised the presidency since 1932. Reflecting this combination of influences, these studies were concerned primarily to explain the prevailing, more or less static distribution of presidential voting preferences in the American public and attributed it to the determinants of the vote being social and long-standing. Thus, the Democratic party owed its hegemonic position to a favourable distribution of social characteristics in the voting public and, moreover, its hegemony could be expected to persist into the foreseeable future since this distribution would not change markedly in the short term.[15] But the Republican candidate's victory in the 1952 presidential election quickly threw the limitations of this perspective into sharp relief. It became seen to provide no clear means of explaining the alternation in electoral outcomes that regularly characterise democratic polities. Researchers were therefore forced to concentrate their minds on the question of electoral change as well as stasis.

The model that was devised to overcome this problem is social-pyschological in perspective. It posits that electoral behaviour is composed of three dimensions: stasis, long-term change and short-term change. Stasis is promoted by the incidence and intensity of party identification, or partisanship, in the electorate. This identification is a pyschological phenomenon that is itself socially determined to some degree. Working class people, for example, are likely to identify with parties of the left simply because of their position of relative social and economic disadvantage in society. Electoral change is a more complex phenomenon and falls into two categories, long- and short-term change in the balance of party support in the electorate. The former is synonymous with a net change in the inter-party balance of partisanship and generally results from either a national crisis that lastingly discredits one or other party in the electorate's eyes or from a more gradual process of social and economic change that is skewed in its impact on the fortunes of the individual parties. Industrialisation is a good example of such change. Clearly different is short-term change, which relates to party votes rather than to party identification and it is the outcome of an unbalanced pattern of temporary voting defections among party identifiers in particular elections. It is short-term precisely because it is random in its long-term effect on the inter-party distribution of the vote. The forces producing such change are candidates and issues and their influence on individuals' choice at the polls combines with that of party identification to produce an aggregate electoral outcome.[16]

This model has provided the conceptual framework for the majority of voting choice studies in the United States and other democracies for the last two decades or so.[17] It owes its popularity and preeminence to three principal assets: (i) it encapsulates the sociological insights regarding the stability of the large part of the electorate's voting habits; (ii) it provides a coherent framework for the explanation of electoral change; and, most importantly from the perspective of this book, (iii) it reinstates elections as inescapably political phenomena through its forceful argument that political parties are not the hapless victims of largely unchanging and immutable social forces when contesting elections. Instead, it holds, through the judicious selection of candidates to run under their banner and of issues to canvass in the campaign, parties can mobilise their own supporters and maybe even convert others to their cause, thereby influencing, perhaps decisively, the outcome of the election. In more general terms, these assets combine to give the model flexibility in adapting to the explanation of changing patterns of electoral behaviour. Increased volatility, for example, can mean that the electorate has become more responsive to short-term forces as the electoral influence of party identification has weakened.[18]

Despite its great popularity over the last two decades or so, however, it remains a model whose fundamental insights have not been fully exploited. Its architects originally intended that it be equally enlightening in the explanation of the dynamics of both voting turnout and voting choice. 'In fundamental respects our approach to the explanation of turnout and partisan choice is the same and the (same) theoretical considerations...have guided our orientation to each of these dimensions of the voting act.'[19] The simple fact of the matter, though, is that the rationale of this model has nowhere guided an analysis of the *interplay* of long- and short-term influences on voting turnout in the same systematic fashion that has been the norm with voting choice studies. Instead, as indicated in the introductory section of this chapter, turnout studies are overwhelmingly characterised by having only a long-term perspective. Even the book expressing an equal theoretical concern for both dimensions of the voting act, *The American Voter*, devotes no more than one full chapter out of twenty to the subject of turnout and then examines it in its relationship to longitudinally stable phenomena like party identification and a sense of political involvement and political efficacy. The ephemeral political dynamism introduced into elections by parties attempting to influence turnout patterns through, say, the nomination of attractive candidates is ignored.[20]

The point, then, is that electoral participation is the poor relation in our efforts to understand the dynamics of the voting act. It is an underdeveloped branch of the study of electoral behaviour precisely because the contribution of short-term forces to the explanation of the variation in turnout, be it at the level of the individual or of some aggregate like the constituency, has been largely ignored. This is most strikingly true with regard to the contribution political parties might make to such an explanation. In an observation that applies equally to elections in other democracies, one recent study of turnout in the United States has summed up the situation as follows:

> Still, a perusal of the work on American politics exposes a rather striking tendency in studies of participation to ignore, or soft pedal, the effects of active political mobilization. Political

scientists create images of voters driven by a sense of effectiveness, by intensely partisan feelings, or by some other psychological involvement; or moved by the skills and resources cultivated in substantial formal education; or pushed toward the polls by a relaxed and easy legal environment. But it is a comparative rarity for students of electoral turnout to credit active efforts by parties and candidates to campaign aggressively and to bring voters to the polls. Yet surely one explanation for variation in electoral participation across individuals or electoral units lies in the amount and intensity of political mobilization - candidates are or are not highly competitive; political parties are or are not well organized and vigorous; campaigning is intense, with abundant advertising in newspapers, exposure on television, bumper stickers, buttons, personal appearances, rallies and leaflets, or it is not.[21]

To make this argument is not to imply that the role played by political parties in getting out the vote has been altogether neglected by political scientists. A number of studies in Britain and the United States especially have spoken to precisely this issue. These, however, are not without their limitations and generally suffer from one or more of the following shortcomings. They tend to focus on one electoral unit or a small number of them rather than on the nation as a whole; they restrict their attention to only one of the several means by which parties might influence turnout patterns, usually campaign expenditure or party activity in the form of canvassing; and, finally, they virtually always look at only one type of election so that little comparative can be said about how parties perform in other types.[22]

The analysis undertaken in this book avoids these shortcomings by having as its frame of reference Britain as a whole, by examining a range of party characteristics that can be expected to influence turnout patterns and, finally, by comparing their influence on turnout in two distinctive types of parliamentary election, general elections and by-elections, as well as on the change in the level of turnout between them.

Research Design

Research Objectives

Two closely related shortcomings have been identified in the extant literature on electoral participation. The first is a failure.

despite the example of numerous voting choice studies, to go beyond the conceptualisation stage in explaining turnout in terms of the interplay between long- and short-term political forces. This failure is due in no small part to the excessive long-term emphasis in empirical studies of this mode of political participation. The all-too-common neglect of short-term forces is responsible for the second shortcoming of turnout studies, which is that they tend to be apolitical in the sense of neglecting the role played by political parties in structuring turnout patterns. Thus, a central function of political parties, the mobilisation of the vote, is understudied and the short-term variation in turnout between electoral units left in an explanatory limbo.

This book represents an effort to overcome both these shortcomings in the context of recent British parliamentary elections. Its focus is the politics of turnout in the sense that it is concerned with the question of how political parties - by virtue of the policy choices they offer, the strategic decisions they make, the candidates they put forward and the standing they enjoy with the electorate - affect constituency turnout patterns in these elections. Parliamentary elections themselves are of two types, general elections and by-elections, which means that turnout in them assumes, potentially at least, a multi-dimensional character. A third dimension is added if the example of voting choice studies is followed and the change in the level of turnout between general and by-elections is treated as a phenomenon worthy of study in its own right. This book will compare and contrast the effect of political parties on all three turnout dimensions and its central hypothesis is that, each having its own distinctive dynamic, the nature of the relationship between party and turnout will vary from one of them to the other.

There is good, *prima facie* evidence for this hypothesis. For a start, research has already established that party efforts to mobilise their vote in the United States are more successful the less important the election in terms of the office at stake. That is, campaign effort increases a party's share of the vote more in local than in presidential elections.[23] While no comparable study exists for Britain, there is no reason to expect the situation to be any different there.[24] The simple fact of the matter is that political parties are not the only agencies whose activities serve to bring people to the polls at election time; others include the mass media, interest groups, voluntary organisations and opinion leaders. Moreover, these competing agencies are more active and influential the more important the election and the more there is at stake in it. General elections see them in full flow because the prize is control of government, whereas the prize in by-elections is relatively minor - loss or gain of a single parliamentary seat. The effect of parties on turnout, in other words, should be more decisive in by-elections since they can be expected to dominate both political activity and the exercise of influence more in this type of election.

There is one situation, of course, in which this argument would not hold and it is the situation in which political parties look on general and by-elections differently and fail to show the same concern to do equally well in both of them. It cannot be doubted that numerous motives drive Britain's political parties to do as well as possible in general elections. The larger of them want to win control of government and the smaller of them to hold the balance of power in a hung Parliament or, more modestly, to influence government policies impinging on the interests of their constituents. All of them need general election success to prevent supporter frustration from threatening their continued existence. By-election success, in contrast, carries few of these prizes in its wake. In particular, their outcome rarely redistributes parliamentary power and influence over government policy. The parties might well be excused, therefore, for viewing by-elections as 'down-market' contests of little ultimate import or consequence. But there is no evidence that this is in fact their view. The National Front apart, they are all parliamentary in ethos and strategy, which means that their principal aim in contesting elections is to win them, or at least to do well enough to enhance their credibility as a viable alternative to the party holding the seat or, more importantly, in government. Governments for their part are just as anxious to do well in them since by-elections are generally, and quite rightly, interpreted as referendums on their performance in office. Poor results in them can erode their public credibility, promote leadership disunity and weaken party morale and confidence.[25]

More concretely, that Britain's parties consider by-elections to be no less important than general elections is apparent from the selection and deployment of their candidates in the two types of election. At least as much care is taken in the selection of by-election candidates if only because 'the national agencies of each party are well aware that a by-election result will be widely regarded as an indication of the party's current popularity...So they want their by-election candidates to be especially attractive to win whatever additional votes personal qualities can win.'[26] Equally, local party organisations take great pains to retain in their own hands the power to nominate a by-election candidate who, in their view, is suited to the needs of, and will have maximum appeal in, the constituency.[27] Nor are 'good' candidates in this regard likely to be available only to the party with the best chance of winning the seat since it is common practice for aspiring Members of Parliament (MPs) to contest an unwinnable seat in order to improve their chance of securing a more favourable nomination the next time around. In the words of a former MP: 'Although a by-election campaign closely resembles that within an individual constituency at a general election, it frequently excites a great deal more interest. There is normally far stronger competition to be selected as a candidate, even for the minority party in a hopeless seat, as the publicity given to the by-election might well result in a subsequent invitation from constituency parties in more attractive seats.'[28]

The importance parties attach to by-elections is also apparent in the pattern of candidatures in parliamentary elections. Minor parties in particular expend resources putting up candidates only when they feel themselves to have a chance of doing well in the contest. Thus, their candidates are found more commonly in by-election than in general election contests in the same constituency since the public's voting habits tend to be less stable and predictable in the former. The Liberal party, for example, fielded a candidate in 43.2 per cent of the general election contests in this analysis, but in 61.2 per cent of by-elections contests. The nationalist parties show a similar bias towards by-elections. The Scottish National party fought 30.8 per cent of this population's 39 Scottish seats in general elections and 56.4 per cent of them in by-elections; the same figures for the Plaid Cymru in the 15 Welsh seats are 66.7 and 93.3 per cent respectively.[29]

Noone doubts, then, that the parties represented in the House of Commons contest general elections with a view to winning as many seats in them as possible. All the evidence indicates that they put up candidates in by-elections with the same aim of winning the seat. There is every reason, therefore, to expect a party effect on by-election as well as general election turnout. The same goes for the remaining turnout dimension, the change between general and by-election. Either because parties win national office through attracting uncommitted and transient supporters or because their supporters become disillusioned with their party when in office, a common belief is that the government's share of the poll suffers disproportionately from the drop in turnout relative to the preceding general election that almost invariably characterises by-elections. 'The feature of the Walthamstow and Brighton by-elections was the abnormally low polls, mainly to be explained by the massive abstentions of Labour voters who have lost faith and hope in the (Labour) Government.'[30] Given this diagnosis of why governments lose votes in by-elections, it seems reasonable to expect the governing party at least to do its best to minimise the drop in the number of its supporters going to the polls between general and by-elections. Moreover, other parties can be expected to follow suit if only to ensure that they are not disadvantaged by the governing party's efforts in this regard.

Up to this point, the primary concern of this chapter has been to justify the hypothesis of a party effect on voting turnout despite the general neglect of this subject in the voluminous literature on electoral participation. It now proceeds to the disaggregation of the notion of a 'party effect' and to the more precise task of identifying ways in which political parties might influence turnout patterns. Specific hypotheses are not articulated partly because the party characteristics structuring turnout patterns could well vary in their effect from one party to another and from one turnout dimension to another and partly because the identification of these characteristics and the specification of the form that their influence takes is properly the domain of empirical enquiry.

In point of fact, the selection of party characteristics to be tested in relation to electoral participation has been guided by two considerations. The first, and more pragmatic, is the availability of suitable data, a consideration dealt with more fully in the next section of this chapter. The second, and theoretically more important, is the literature on voting turnout in particular and the voting act in general. The characteristics themselves have been grouped into three internally coherent clusters, with each cluster forming the basis of a separate analysis and chapter in the book. In order of their presentation, these clusters profile: (i) the political context of the election; (ii) the party candidates in the constituency; and (iii) the standing in countrywide public opinion of the national parties and their leaders. These clusters represent the short-term electoral forces at the core of this book. Although there is some interrelationship between them, they are always treated separately in order to make the analysis more manageable and readily comprehensible. Since this analysis juxtaposes long- and short-term political determinants of turnout, its basic strategy is to regress each turnout dimension on each of the three clusters *plus* the long-term forces alluded to earlier in this chapter and described more fully in Chapter 2. Multiple regression is the analytical technique chosen for this enterprise because it has a number of desirable qualities. First, its multivariate character permits the estimation of the relative importance of a number of explanatory variables through the comparison of their beta weight values. Second, it potentially reduces the number of statistically (and, for the purposes of this analysis, theoretically) significant explanatory variables. Finally, it can identify explanatory variables which may, in bivariate terms, show no relationship with the dependent variables, but which may do so once the confounding effects of the other explanatory variables are controlled.

The long- and short-term political variables are the only ones to figure explicitly in the analysis undertaken in this book, although this is not to imply that they are the only ones likely to affect constituency turnout patterns. A number of constituencies' socioeconomic characteristics might also prove to have an effect if built into the regression equation. The more suburban a constituency, for example, the higher will be the turnout in both types of parliamentary election. Conversely, turnout tends to be lower in inner-city seats. Unfortunately, though, constituency characteristics of this type cannot be included in this analysis since official government publications aggregate them by constituency only from the 1966 sample census onwards. This means that they are not available for around 60 per cent of the by-election constituencies in this analysis (see Appendix A).

Moreover, there are three reasons why their absence should not be considered a particularly serious problem. In the first place, the explicit focus of this analysis is the politics of turnout and to include in it non-political variables would only risk obfuscating this focus unnecessarily. The two remaining reasons relate to why there is little need to run such a risk. Broadly speaking, the aim of this analysis is to assess and compare the short-term effect of political parties on various dimensions of parliamentary election turnout. Exogenous factors will distort this comparison only if their value changes substantially between the parliamentary elections at hand. This is extremely unlikely with constituencies' socioeconomic characteristics since these change slowly at best. By-elections, in sharp contrast, follow relatively quickly on the heels of general elections; the average time separating them in post-war Britain is a little less than two and a quarter years. Finally, and relatedly, some of the effect of constituency socioeconomic characteristics will be a function of population mobility and its effect on the electoral register. Turnout is high in the suburbs because, in contrast to inner city dwellers, suburban residents are more likely to own their own home, to have family commitments and career jobs and generally to be more settled and part of an established community.[31] Their lesser residential mobility means that suburban registers remain more accurate as they age and turnout is not artificially deflated to the same extent as a result of being estimated against a list containing the names of people no longer living in the constituency. Chapter 3 shows that once a range of other political factors is statistically controlled, the register age's negative effect on turnout disappears.

Design Problems

Any research project will find itself confronted with two types of difficulty. The first relates to problems of conceptualisation and design and the second to technical difficulties like multicollinearity and outliers. This section is concerned with the first type since these constitute the more fundamental issues that determine the worth or otherwise of any project. Technical difficulties will be dealt with as they crop up in the course of the analysis.

A distinct advantage of this analysis is that any problems that it might have do not arise from conceptual difficulties since the individual variables comprising it are straightforwardly operationalised and interpreted. Better measures of some of the concepts might well be conceivable in principle, but at least no serious reliability or validity problems arise with the measures used. This is not to argue, however, that the analysis could not be improved, especially if more senstive data were available. The problems besetting it are common to aggregate data studies generally and stem directly from its total dependence on this one kind of data. Nor is this dependence a matter of choice. Rather, it is made inevitable by one of the book's unique features, the comparison of general and by-elections. Individual-level data are available for all British general elections from 1964 onwards, but, to the best of my knowledge, similar data from the constituencies in which by-elections have been held are not available in the public domain; there have certainly been no academic by-election studies to match the general election ones. Thus, systematic, individual-level comparison across the two types of election is impossible.

The study's first shortcoming, then, is that it gives no consideration to the short-term, attitudinal correlates of voting turnout. This is to to be regretted since there is ample evidence to suggest that these complement long-term, aggregate characteristics in the explanation of variation in constituency turnout patterns. Controlling on a number of long-term variables like party identification, political interest, class and education, for example, one recent study of electoral participation in contests for the US presidency has demonstrated that '(i)n general, if one has a clear choice among the candidates (is not indifferent) and one's policy preferences are close to at least one candidate (one is not alienated), one is much more likely to vote'.[32] In other words, the electorate's evaluations of the candidates on offer to them in particular elections can decisively influence their decision of whether or not to vote even after a host of long-term factors usually invoked to explain voting has been taken into account.

The absence of attitudinal analysis is more accurately described as a weakness in the design rather than as a problem with it; the aggregate analysis remains an entirely worthwhile and legitimate enterprise. A problem does arise, however, with the use of a single dependent variable, constituencywide voting turnout, throughout the analysis. There are no complications when this variable is related to other constituency or by-election characteristics in Chapter 3, but there are when it is associated with individual candidate and party characteristics in Chapters 4 and 5. The essence of this problem is that constituency turnout is a relatively insensitive measure of party effect and it is so because political parties are instrumental organisations that seek to mobilise their own potential supporters within constituencies rather than constituency electorates as a whole. Moreover, it is possible for them to be successful in this regard, but for it not to show up in the constituencywide analysis. An attractive Conservative candidate, for example, might bring more Conservative supporters to the polls, while simultaneously encouraging an equal number of other parties' supporters to stay at home as a result of having sown a sense of defeatism in their ranks. But despite his having had a very real impact on turnout patterns, no candidate effect would manifest itself in the aggregate.

While undoubtedly there, it is easy to overstate the magnitude of this problem, however. On the one hand and taking the same example, the form that the problem will take is more likely to be to underestimate candidate effect rather than to miss it altogether since movement into and out of abstention among individual groups of supporters will rarely be so well balanced as to be self-cancelling. Of course, the pattern of movements that produce the net effect will not be decipherable from aggregate data, but this does not gainsay the candidate's influence on turnout in the constituency at large. On the other hand, we are not altogether helpless before this problem. Some more precise idea of the explanatory role of candidates and parties can be gained by looking at their relationship to turnout patterns in different types of constituency. This is one of the reasons (other, more idiosyncratic ones are elaborated in the individual chapters) for disaggregating the population of by-election constituencies into Labour versus Conservative and government versus opposition seats in each of Chapters 3, 4 and 5. While not circumventing the basic problem of decipherability, this strategy of disaggregation does have the advantage of highlighting coherent and readily interpretable differences between these seat groupings.

A more serious shortcoming of the analysis is that it contains no direct measure of the organisational mobilisation of the vote at the level of the constituency. The obvious candidates for such a measure are each party's membership or campaign expenditure in the constituency, but complete data on neither are available. To take party membership figures, 'only the Labour party publishes such information, and it sets a minimum of one thousand members for affiliated parties. In both 1966 and 1970 most local Labour Parties claimed to have exactly one thousand members, which makes the data almost impossible to interpret'.[33] Campaign expenditure is more promising since candidates' general election expenses are published in parliamentary reports covering individual elections. The same expenditure data for by-elections, though, 'are hard to come by (and) must be far more misleading than those for general elections. In a key contest the amount of effort put in by party headquarters, including on occasion expensive market research and large numbers of paid agents, could be costed at a substantially higher value than all the local activities duly recorded in the expense return.'[34]

Again, however, the problem turns out on consideration not to be as serious as it first appears. There is ample enough evidence from Britain and elsewhere to leave nobody in any doubt that the greater the mobilisation effort in an election, the higher the turnout. Equally, there can be no doubt that this relationship is very strong, perhaps strong enough to overwhelm other short-term political influences on turnout. In the absence of a direct measure of organisation, therefore, an adequate, if second-best, strategy is to aim less at accurately estimating its effect and more at determining whether other variables have an influence once its *likely* effect (as measured by a surrogate variable) is controlled. Other strong relationships that then emerge can be accepted with confidence. The key to this strategy is, of course, to find a reliable surrogate measure of the organisational mobilisation of the constituency vote. Since this section of the book is more concerned to show an awareness of methodological shortcomings than it is to specify in detail how they will be dealt with, now is not the time to present and justify the choice of surrogate. This particular task will be addressed when the analysis proper gets underway in Chapter 3.

Format of Presentation

From Chapter 2 onwards, this book can be divided into three parts, the first consisting of Chapter 2, the second of Chapters 3, 4 and 5 and the third of Chapter 6.

Chapter 2 essentially provides the descriptive background to the subsequent analysis of the political determinants of constituency turnout patterns. It starts with a brief description of how the two types of parliamentary election are called and defines the temporal and spatial parameters of the analysis to follow. This is followed by a descriptive profile of the three dimensions of parliamentary election turnout, which highlights a number of interesting and important differences between them. Again as part of the background to the primary focus on short-term forces, the final section of the chapter deals with the identification and measurement of their long-term counterparts. Falling into two categories, those common to all democracies and those unique to Britain, long-term forces are of interest both in their own right and because their effect has to be controlled to gain an independent estimate of the effect of the various short-term forces.

Chapters 3 to 5 constitute the substantively important part of the book since it is in these that the politics of turnout is investigated in detail. Differing only in their substantive focus (i.e., in the cluster of short-term forces that each investigates), these three chapters follow the same organisational format. Although treated separately, the clusters of determinants should not be viewed as being rigidly independent of each other. Rather, their separation is better viewed as a necessary simplifying device and the conceptual overlap between them is explicitly recognised in the analysis by the electoral marginality variable appearing in each chapter. Equally, however, the degree of their overlap should not be overstated; the clusters do enjoy an unambiguous internal coherence and do reflect analytically and logically separable aspects of party influence.

Common to the three substantive chapters is an introductory section setting out the rationale for the hypothesis of a relationship between the particular cluster of party characteristics and voting turnout patterns. Then comes the identification of the individual party characteristics comprising that chapter's cluster, an elaboration of why they can each be expected to be related to constituency turnout and how they are each operationalised. The third and fourth sections of Chapters 3, 4 and 5 are the substantively important ones because it is in them that the findings of the analysis are presented, discussed and interpreted. The third section deals with the level of turnout in general and by-elections and the fourth with the rate of change of turnout between them. The concluding section of each chapter attempts to provide an integrated overview of its most important findings.

The final part of the book is made up of the concluding chapter and there the conclusions from the individual chapters about the impact of long- and short-term forces are integrated into a more general discussion of the influence of political parties on constituency turnout patterns.

Notes

[1]Sidney Verba and Norman H. Nie, *Participation in America: Political Democracy and Social Equality* (New York: Harper and Row, 1972), pp. 2-3.See also Sidney Verba, Norman H. Nie and Jae-on Kim, *Participation and Political Equality: A Seven-Nation Comparison* (Cambridge: Cambridge University Press, 1978). This is democratic participation, of course. Popular participation in more authoritarian societies is encouraged not to influence government, but to demonstrate passive support for the regime through staged events like mass rallies, plebiscites and elections without choice. 'Support' participation of this type has been alternatively termed 'coercive mobilization'. See Myron Weiner, 'Political Participation' in Leonard Binder et al., *Crises and Sequences in Political Development* (Princeton, N.J.: Princeton University Press, 1971), pp. 164-65.

[2]See Robert E. Lane, *Political Life: Why and How People Get Involved in Politics* (New York: Free Press, 1959) and Lester W. Milbrath and M.L. Goel, *Political Participation*, 2nd ed. (Chicago: Rand McNally, 1977).

[3]The seminal statement of this argument is Anthony Downs, *An Economic Theory of Democracy* (New York: Harper and Row, 1957).

[4]Paul Kleppner, *Who Voted? The Dynamics of Electoral Turnout, 1870-1980* (New York: Praeger, 1982), p. 5. For similar data on Britain, see David Butler and Donald Stokes, *Political Change in Britain*, 2nd ed. (London: Macmillan, 1974), p. 21.

[5]This is a quotation by Samuel P. Huntington and it appears in Guy Hermet, 'State-Controlled Elections: A Framework' in Guy Hermet, Richard Rose and Alain Rouquie, eds, *Elections Without Choice* (London: Macmillan, 1978), p. 213. For a more general discussion of the relationship between mass political participation and various democratic theories, see Carole Pateman, *Participation and Democratic Theory* (Cambridge: Cambridge University Press, 1970).

[6]See Seymour Martin Lipset, *Political Man*, expanded ed. (London: Heinemann, 1983), pp. 183-230 and Milbrath and Goel, *Political Participation, passim.*

[7]Raymond E. Wolfinger and Steven J. Rosenstone, *Who Votes?* (New Haven: Yale University Press, 1980), p. 102.

[8]A good overview is G. Bingham Powell, Jr., 'Voting Turnout in Thirty Democracies: Partisan, Legal, and Socio-Economic Influences' in Richard Rose, ed., *Electoral Participation* (London: Sage, 1980), pp. 20-29. See also Powell's, *Contemporary Democracies* (Cambridge, Mass.: Harvard University Press, 1983).

[9]See Angus Campbell, Gerald Gurin and Warren E. Miller, *The Voter Decides* (Evanston, Ill.: Row, Peterson, 1954) and Angus Campbell, Philip E. Converse, Warren E. Miller and Donald E. Stokes. *The American Voter* (New York: Wiley, 1960).

[10]See Gabriel A. Almond and Sidney Verba, *The Civic Culture: Political Attitudes and Democracy in Five Nations* (Princeton, N.J.: Princeton University Press, 1963) and Norman H. Nie, G. Bingham Powell and Kenneth Prewitt, 'Social Structure and Political Participation: Developmental Relationships', *American Political Science Review*, 63 (1969), 361-78 and 808-32.

[11]Stein Rokkan, 'The Comparative Study of Political Participation' in Austin Ranney, ed., *Essays in the Behavioral Study of Politics* (Urbana: University of Illinois Press, 1962); Stein Rokkan and Angus Campbell, 'Citizen Participation in Political Life: Norway and the United States of America', *International Social Science Journal*, 12 (1960), 69-99; and Stein Rokkan and Henry Valen, 'The Mobilization of the Periphery', *Acta Sociologica*, 6 (1962), 111-58. Earlier noteworthy studies of this type include Charles E. Merriam and Harold F. Gosnell, *Non-Voting: Causes and Methods of Control* (Chicago: University of Chicago Press, 1924) and Herbert Tingsten, *Political Behaviour* (London: P.S. King, 1937).

[12]See Ivor Crewe, 'Electoral Participation' in David Butler, Howard R. Penniman and Austin Ranney, eds, *Democracy at the Polls* (Washington D.C.: American Enterprise Institute, 1981), pp. 239-53.

[13]Wolfinger and Rosenstone, *Who Votes?*, p. 88. For a similar analysis and conclusion across countries, see Powell, 'Voting Turnout in Thirty Democracies', pp. 26-29.

[14]See L.F. Crisp, *Australian National Government*, 4th ed., (Melbourne: Longman Cheshire, 1978), pp. 142-43 and Galen Irwin, 'Compulsory Voting Legislation: Impact on Voter Turnout in the Netherlands', *Comparative Political Studies*, 7 (1974), 292-315.

[15]See Paul F. Lazarsfeld, Bernard R. Berelson and Hazel Gaudet, *The People's Choice* (New York: Duell, Sloan and Pearce, 1944) and Bernard R. Berelson, Paul F. Lazarsfeld and William N. McPhee, *Voting* (Chicago: University of Chicago Press, 1954). Good British examples of this genre are R.S. Milne and H.C. Mackenzie, *Straight Fight* (London: The Hansard Society, 1954 and *idem, Marginal Seat* (London: The Hansard Society, 1958).

[16]This model is pioneered in Campbell et al., *The Voter Decides* and Campbell et al., *The American Voter*. It is excellently summarised in Kenneth Prewitt and Norman H. Nie, 'Election Studies of the Survey Research Center', *British Journal of Political Science*, 1 (1971), 479-502.

[17]See Herbert B. Asher, 'Voting Behavior Research in the 1980s: An Examination of Some Old and New Problem Areas' and Ronald Inglehart, 'Changing Paradigms in Comparative Political Behavior', both of which are in Ada W. Finifter, ed., *Political Science: The State of the Discipline* (Washington D.C.: American Political Science Association, 1983), 339-88 and 429-69.

[18]This is a central theme running through the country studies in Ivor Crewe and David Denver, eds, *Electoral Change in Western Democracies:*

Patterns and Sources of Electoral Volatility (London: Croom Helm, 1985).

[19]Campbell et al., *The American Voter*, p. 90.

[20]Campbell et al., *The American Voter*, ch. 5. A similar emphasis can also be found in studies of countries other than the United States. See, for example, Ivor Crewe, Tony Fox and Jim Alt, 'Non-Voting in British General Elections 1966 - October 1974', in Colin Crouch, ed., *British Political Sociology Yearbook, vol. 3: Participation in Politics* (London: Croom Helm, 1977), pp. 50-79 and M. Kent Jennings, 'Partisan Commitment and Electoral Behavior in the Netherlands', *Acta Sociologica*, 7 (1972), 445-70.

[21]Samuel C. Patterson and Gregory A. Caldeira, 'Getting Out the Vote: Participation in Gubernatorial Elections', *American Political Science Review*, 77 (1983), p. 677.

[22]For the United States, see Patterson and Caldeira, 'Getting Out the Vote' and the literature cited therein. For Britain, see P.J. Taylor and R.J. Johnston, *Geography of Elections* (Harmondsworth: Penguin, 1979), pp. 305-32 and the literature cited therein.

[23]See William J. Crotty, 'Party Effort and the Impact on the Vote', *American Political Science Review*, 65 (1971), 439-50.

[24]There have been studies of the effect of party activity in a single type of election and these include John M. Bochel and David T. Denver, 'Canvassing, Turnout and Party Support', *British Journal of Political Science*, 4 (1974), 17-35 for local elections and A.H. Taylor, 'The Effect of Party Organization: Correlation Between Campaign Expenditure and Voting in the 1970 Election', *Political Studies*, 20 (1972), 329-31 for general elections.

[25]See Anthony Mughan, 'Towards a Political Explanation of Government Vote Losses in Midterm By-Elections', *American Political Science Review*, 80 (1986).

[26]Austin Ranney, *Pathways to Parliament: Candidate Selection in Britain* (London: Macmillan, 1965), p. 35. See also Michael Rush, *The Selection of Parliamentary Candidates* (London: Nelson, 1969).

[27]A good example of local party power in this regard is Peter Tatchell, Labour's candidate for the Bermondsey by-election of 24 February 1983. The Labour leader, Michael Foot, declared publicly that Tatchell would never be endorsed by the national party because of his views on extra-parliamentary action. In the end, however, Mr. Foot 'had to give way before a local party determined to retain Mr. Tatchell'. See David Butler and Dennis Kavanagh, *The British General Election of 1983* (London: Macmillan, 1984), p. 59.

[28]R.L. Leonard, *Elections in Britain* (London: Van Nostrand, 1968), p. 120. A recent analysis of MPs' previous experience as parliamentary candidates is Anthony King, 'The Rise of the Career Politician in Britain - And its Consequences', *British Journal of Political Science*, 11 (1981), 249-86.

[29]These figures are calculated over all 294 contests.

[30]*The Times*, 28 March 1969, p. 1. For academic statements of the same thesis, see Angus Campbell, 'Surge and Decline: A Study of Electoral Change' in Angus Campbell, Philip E. Converse, Warren E. Miller and Donald E. Stokes, *Elections and the Political Order* (New York: Wiley, 1966) and Anthony King, 'Why All Governments Lose by-Elections', *New Society*, 21 March, 1968, 413-15. For a dissenting view, however, see Mughan, 'Towards a Political Explanation'.

[31]One individual-level study of turnout in British general elections has concluded: 'It is social isolation, therefore, not social deprivation, to which non-voting or at least irregular voting, should be attributed.' See Crewe et al., 'Non-Voting in British General Elections', p. 63.

[32]John F. Zipp, 'Perceived Representativeness and Voting: An Assessment of the Impact of "Choices" vs. "Echoes"', *American Political Science Review*, 79 (1985), p. 58. Although its focus is exclusively on long-term variables, a study combining aggregate- and individual-level data is Jae-On Kim, John R. Petrocik and Stephen N. Enokson, 'Voter Turnout Among the American States: Systemic and Individual Components', *American Political Science Review*, 69 (1975), 107-23.

[33]Taylor, 'The Effect of Party Organization', pp. 329-30.

[34]David Butler, 'By-Elections and their Interpretation' in Chris Cook and John Ramsden, eds, *By-Elections in British Politics* (London: Macmillan, 1973), p. 6.

The Institutional Framework

Electors in the United Kingdom are periodically called to the polls to fill the various elective offices in local and national government. It is only national elections that are of concern to this study and their immediate function is to allow individual voters, grouped into constituencies, to elect someone to represent them in Parliament, specifically the House of Commons. These representatives themselves then elect a government, which is usually constituted wholly from within their own ranks. National, or parliamentary, elections are not held on a fixed date, although there is an upper limit to the time that can elapse before the next one is called. In 1694, this limit was set at three years, only to be increased to seven in 1715. The promulgation of the Parliament Act of 1911 then reduced this figure to five years. That limit persists to this day and the only exceptions to it this century have been the governments elected in 1910 and 1935, both of which stayed in office beyond the statutory limit because of the special circumstances of two world wars. Otherwise, no peacetime government has even completed its full five-year term of office. The one to come closest to it was the Conservative government that was elected in 1959; it remained in office for just twenty-four days less than its full term.

The basic reason elections are so often held prematurely is that the leader of Parliament, the Prime Minister, has the right to recommend to the Monarch that a Parliament be dissolved at any point in its lifetime and it is rare for such a recommendation not to be acted upon. As soon as is practicable after Parliament has been dissolved, a writ is issued to the local returning officer in each constituency and the elections for a new Parliament get under way more or less immediately thereafter.

This is the procedure for calling general elections, the distinguishing characteristic of which is their simultaneous election of the full complement of Members of Parliament (MPs). Twelve such elections have been held in the United Kingdom since the end of the Second World War; the years of their occurrence are 1945,

1950, 1951, 1955, 1959, 1964, 1966, 1970, February 1974, October 1974, 1979 and 1983. As noted, all were held before Parliament's full term had expired and numerous factors influenced Prime Ministers in their decision to 'go to the country'. The most obvious of them is the receipt of only a small parliamentary majority in the previous general election; this was the predicament that occasioned the rapid return to the polls of 1951, 1966 and October 1974. Other, less tangible reasons include the economic situation, the state of the Government's legislative programme in the House of Commons and the need for the country to be represented at important international negotiations by a government with a fresh vote of confidence from the people. Additional factors could be cited, but the most succinct, if perhaps oversimplistic, explanation for general elections being called prematurely remains that of the Conservative party's joint chairman in 1963: 'The Prime Minister is likely to have a general election when he thinks he is most likely to win it'.[1]

Although easily the more common way of doing so, general elections are not the only means by which House of Commons seats are filled. There is a second type of parliamentary election, the constituency by-election, whose immediate function is to fill casual vacancies that arise within the lifetime of a Parliament. In other words, by-elections involve the choice of a single MP rather than the whole House of Commons and become necessary when individual sitting members vacate the seat to which they were elected in the last general election. The causes of such vacancies are several and they will be touched upon presently (see Table 2.1). For the moment, however, a brief description of the procedure for calling by-elections is in order since it has a direct bearing on Chapter 3's assessment of the importance of their timing.

The writ ordaining a by-election is issued not by Royal Proclamation, but by the Speaker of the House of Commons after the appropriate motion has been moved on the floor of the House. The by-election is then held some two to three weeks later. In practice, however, its actually being called can be delayed for a substantial time since, by tradition, it is the Whips of the party holding the seat who move the writ in Parliament. Especially if this party is in government, any number of tactical considerations might dictate that the writ is best delayed. The result is that casual vacancies are quite often left unfilled for up to six months. The minimum period for filling them, on the other hand, is about six weeks.[2]

The purpose of this book is to explore how political parties can influence the dynamics of voter turnout both within and between the two types of parliamentary election. But before it can be systematically undertaken, the analysis' parameters have to be defined. The first of these parameters is the temporal one, i.e., the time period to be covered. Since it was the end of the Second World War that ushered in the class-based alignment underpinning the current electoral hegemony of the Conservative and Labour parties, the 1945 general election might seem the most appropriate starting point.[3] The only difficulty is that this election retained a number of pre-war characteristics that were only abolished with the 1948 Representation of the People Act. The most prominent of these characteristics were double-member University constituencies and plural voting for university graduates and occupiers of business premises. Having been fought strictly on the 'one man, one vote' principle, the 1950 election is commonly held to be the first 'normal' one and, as such, constitutes the starting point of this analysis. Its finishing point is the arbitrary one of the most recent general election, that of 1983.

The second parameter is spatial. The years since 1950 have seen 310 by-elections take place in the United Kingdom, fourteen of which were held in Northern Ireland. But this province's cleavage structure and party system are so different from the class-based British one that the Northern Irish constituencies had to be excluded from further consideration. This leaves a total of 296 by-elections contests in Great Britain (England, Scotland and Wales) between the 1950 and 1983 general elections. The very special circumstances surrounding two of them, Bristol, South-East in August 1963 and Southampton, Itchen in May 1971, dictate that these also be comprehensively dropped from further consideration, leaving the 294 cases that form the core of the investigation to follow.[4] These by-elections are listed chronologically in Appendix A.

Table 2.1 breaks down this population of by-elections by number and cause in each of the ten Parliaments that sat from 1950 to 1983. Its most striking feature is the sharp decline in the absolute number of them held in, roughly speaking, the second half of this period. Their total was 180 in the sixteen years or so spanning the 1950 and 1966 general elections inclusive; this figure then dipped sharply to 113 over more or less the same length of time following the 1966 election and ending in 1983. Nor should it be thought that the higher total in the earlier period is some function of the increase in the number of parliamentary seats from 625 to 630 in the redistribution that followed the 1951 election. After all, there was an

Table 2.1: Number and cause of by-elections by Parliament, 1950-83

			Cause			
Parliament	*Death*	*Resignation*	*Elevation to Peerage*	*Succession to Peerage*	*Expulsion*	*Total*
1950-51	07	06	01			14
1951-55	17	15	10	1	1	44
1955-59	23	11	12	3		49
1959-64	27	17	13	3		60
1964-66	05	03	05			13
1966-70	27	10				37
1970-74(F)	17	10	01	1		29
1974(F)-74(0)			01			01
1974(0)-79	17	09	04			30
1979-83	12	04	01			17
Total	152	85	48	8	1	294

increase of exactly the same size after the 1970 election.

Numerous factors have contributed to this decline and two of them are readily apparent from the second feature of Table 2.1, namely its enumeration of the causes of by-elections. In the first place, fewer MPs die whilst still in Parliament, largely because their average age has gone down. Relatedly, members now also tend to retire earlier.[5] Secondly, far fewer sitting members have been elevated to the peerage since 1966. This is the partly the consequence of the Labour party's having spent more time in office during this latter period and of its greater reluctance to use the political honours system to 'promote' elderly MPs to the House of Lords. More significantly, though, it is also partly the consequence of both major parties having become far more reluctant, especially when in government, to take any action, including elevation to the peerage, that would bring a by-election in its wake. This reluctance stems directly from the stunning vote and seat losses that governments of both parties have suffered in by-elections, losses that have dissuaded them from too readily putting their credibility and popularity to the all-too-public test of the ballot box.[6]Indeed, by-elections have become best known for their manifestation of an anti-government backlash that has become their hallmark in both the academic and popular mind.[7]Not surprisingly given these circumstances, successive British governments' reluctance to risk likely humiliation at the polls is the third, and probably most important, reason for the decline in the incidence of by-elections after 1966.

There seems to be no good reason to hypothesise the existence of a relationship between the cause of, and level of turnout in, by-elections. The purpose of the preceding section has been simply to convey the institutional and political background to the analysis of turnout patterns that is the concern of the remainder of this book. It would therefore now seem appropriate to elaborate the background material already presented and provide a detailed descriptive profile of post-1950 patterns of voting turnout in British general and by-elections.

Patterns of Turnout

A necessary preliminary to the presentation of this profile of the pattern of parliamentary election turnout between 1950 and 1983 concerns the measurement of voting turnout. At first sight, this task presents no problems - voting turnout is operationally defined as the proportion of the eligible electorate actually casting its ballot. A slight complication arises with regard to the demarcation of the eligible electorate, however. In the particular context of Britain, the universe of those eligible to vote is defined by the names found on the constituency electoral register at the time the election in question is called. But being compiled each October and issued in mid-February, this register is already out-of-date by the time it comes into effect and it becomes ever more incomplete as the months elapse until it is renewed. The simple fact of the matter is that a considerable number of people die or move away from a constituency over the course of a year or more. It might be argued, therefore, that a more accurate estimate of turnout would take account of the register's erosion.[8]But there are two reasons why no such adjustment need be made in this analysis. First, being correlated at 0.97 for general elections and 0.98 in by-elections, the unadjusted and adjusted measures are interchangeable for statistical purposes. Second, as a check, the age of the register will figure as an independent variable in its own right in Chapter 3 when the effect on turnout of various aspects of governments' timing of elections will be examined.

Table 2.2 details the general and by-election turnout levels for

Table 2.2: Percentage voting turnout in British parliamentary elections, 1950-83

General elections		By-elections	
1950	84.1	1950-51	68.8
1951	82.7	1951-55	58.9
1955	76.9	1955-59	63.5
1959	79.0	1959-64	64.4
1964	77.2	1964-66	64.4
1966	76.1	1966-70	62.1
1970	71.8	1970-74(F)	56.8
1974(F)	79.1	1974(F)-74(O)	25.9
1974(O)	73.0	1974(O)-79	57.6
1979	76.2	1979-83	56.6
1983	72.7		

each Parliament and a prominent feature of it is the change in the pattern of turnout over time. The high turnout in the the 1950 and 1951 general elections is best treated as an aberration. If its subsequent level is compared to that in elections prior to 1950, the post-1951 decline can be seen to be more apparent than real.[9] There is thus no evidence of a secular trend, positive or negative, in the level of turnout in either general or by-elections. Trend there may not be, but there is an unmistakeable change centring around the decade of the 1970s; it is in 1970 that general election turnout drops appreciably and immediately afterwards that by-election turnout follows suit. Essentially, what happens is that what might be called institutionalised turnout drops a few percentage points in this election and remains on this lower plane thereafter. The mean figure for the 1955, 1959, 1964 and 1966 elections is 77.3 per cent, while for the five after 1966 it is 74.6 per cent. This drop is even sharper for by-elections. Discounting the 1950-51 Parliament, their mean level of turnout falls from 62.7 per cent in the subsequent four Parliaments to 57.0 per cent in the post-1970 period. (This latter figure excludes the February to October 1974 Parliament because of the abnormally low turnout in the one by-election held over its course.)

Perhaps most significant about Table 2.2, however, is the preliminary insights it offers into the nature of the relationship between the two types of election. There is a temptation to dismiss by-elections as 'mini' general elections in which the same immutable forces are at work on the electorate, even if usually at a lesser intensity. In other words, the assumption is that British electoral politics have become nationalised to the extent where, even in by-elections, local forces play at best a peripheral role in dictating trends in party choice and voting turnout.[10]But this assumption would be erroneous. The evidence clearly indicates that by-elections are misleadingly conceptualised if thought of as a pale reflection of general elections; they in fact have their own distinctive character and impetus. To be sure, Table 2.2 shows turnout in the two types of election to move roughly in tandem, but the relationship is far from symbiotic. Both sets of figures, for example, may show a slight downward trend after the 1951 and 1966 elections, yet in both cases the drop is sharper and more sustained for by-election turnout. Even more convincing evidence of their distinctiveness is to be found outside the table. Were the two types of election but different sides of the same coin, voting turnout would be expected to vary approximately equally across constituencies in both of them. But their respective coefficients of variation being 0.19 and 0.09, it transpires that by-election turnout is substantially more variable, which immediately suggests the hypothesis of a more influential role for constituency-specific forces in by-elections.[11] Similarly, despite being further apart in time, turnout in the preceding general election is more highly correlated with that in the succeeding general election (0.72) than with that in the by-election (0.63).[12]In short, by-election turnout has a dynamic that is sufficiently distinctive from that of general elections to merit separate consideration and analysis. Moreover, with a coefficient of variation of 0.63, this conclusion holds even more forcefully for the rate of change of turnout between the two types of election.

The immediate relevance of this conclusion is its confirmation that turnout in both general and by-elections, as well as the change between them, must be investigated separately if there is to be genuine insight into the dynamics of electoral participation. It is appropriate, therefore, that Table 2.2 now be complemented with a similar profile of the rate of change of turnout between the two types of election.

Table 2.3 presents the mean change in turnout from general to by-election for each Parliament. The figures have been calculated by subtracting the latter from the former so that the positive sign indicates that the level of turnout drops in by-elections. The size of this drop, however, can be seen to remain more or less constant over the whole period. Discounting the idiosyncratic, single contest in the February-October 1974 Parliament, it is at its largest after the

Table 2.3: Percentage rate of change of voting turnout in British parliamentary elections, 1950-83

	Rate of change of turnout		
1950-51	16.2	1966-70	12.6
1951-55	22.2	1970-74(F)	12.1
1955-59	12.6	1974(F)-74(O)	37.3
1959-64	14.1	1974(O)-79	12.8
1964-66	11.8	1979-83	14.6

abnormally high turnout in the 1950 and 1951 general elections. Thereafter, there is no sign of a secular trend. Moreover, unlike with cross-sectional turnout (see Table 2.1), neither the 1970 election nor any other heralds a sustained departure of any magnitude from past trends in the rate of change of turnout. This figure averages out at 12.8 per cent for the four Parliaments between 1955 and 1970 inclusive and 13.2 per cent for the 1970-74(F) ones onwards (excluding that of February to October 1974). The most striking feature of Table 2.3, therefore is just how apparently inevitable and how substantial in volume this drop normally is. Indeed, in only fifteen, or 5.1 per cent, of the 294 cases did the proportion of the eligible electorate going to the polls actually rise in the by-election relative to the preceding general election. So rare are these deviant cases that to examine them in a little more detail provides some initial insights into the dynamics of voting turnout.

Their most salient characteristic is their geographical unrepresentativeness. Of the fifteen cases, seven, or 46.6 per cent, are to be found in Scotland and four, or 26.6 per cent, in each of England and Wales.[13] This distribution is heavily skewed away from an England that in fact accounts for 82 per cent of all the by-elections held over the period of this analysis and towards a Scotland and Wales that together hosted only 18 per cent of them. A discrepancy as marked as this one merits later consideration as a long-term determinant whose influence should be controlled when estimating the effects of short-term forces.

The second salient characteristic of these fifteen cases concerns the apparent role of third parties in boosting by-election turnout. In only two of these fifteen contests did the Liberal or Scottish or

Welsh nationalist parties not either intervene anew in the by-election or considerably improve their vote share relative to the preceding general election. 'Intervention' was the more common booster in the early part of the post-war period since parties other than Conservative and Labour fought parliamentary elections only in selected constituencies and 'improvement' the more common when minor parties later came to put up candidates on a far wider scale. Moreover, of the remaining two cases, Carmarthen and Grimsby, the former is highly idiosyncratic in the sense that it involved an former Liberal MP of long standing, Lady Megan Lloyd George, contesting and winning the marginal seat as a Labour candidate. Similarly, the increased turnout in Grimsby could well be attributable, at least in part, to the Labour party candidate, Austin Mitchell; he was a very well-known and popular television broadcaster at the time.[14] Whatever the precise circumstances of these two cases, however, it is clear that the number of candidates is a variable whose potential for influence it would be unwise to ignore. It will figure as a contextual variable in Chapter 3.

In sum, then, this profile has emphasised the analytical distinctiveness of turnout patterns in general and by-elections. In both instances, the level of turnout drops after the 1966 election, but the dip is sharper and more sustained for by-elections. This difference strengthens the conclusion, already suggested by other evidence, that turnout in the two types of election does not respond to the same 'laws'. To complicate matters still further, it is a conclusion that applies equally to the rate of change of turnout from general to by-election. The task that now rears its head is the explanation of this variation. Therefore, the next section of this chapter sets the background for the detailed analysis of short-term forces that is to come by detailing the relationship between their long-term counterparts and the level and rate of change of constituency turnout. The remaining chapters will then assess the contribution of political parties to the explanation of variation in constituency turnout patterns.

Long-Term Determinants of Turnout

Long-term forces are best thought of as background influences whose magnitude remains relatively constant across elections; they are not necessarily immobile but change marginally at best from one election to the next. Such forces fall into two categories, those common to all liberal democracies and those specific to one or other of them.

Being concerned to establish the general theoretical background to this study of Britain, Chapter 1 concentrated its attention on the first of these categories and identified partisanship as the preeminent cross-national and long-term determinant of both voting turnout and party choice. At the individual level, partisanship, or party identification, is a measure of an elector's psychological commitment to a political party. Extrapolated to the systemic level, this logic dictates that aggregate partisanship be conceptualised in terms of the commitment of social groups to political parties.

> (W)here strong linkages exist between national parties, or blocs of parties, and demographic groups, voting participation should be encouraged...Where these linkages are relatively stable, they provide cues to even poorly informed and less interested voters as to the interpretation of issue and candidate choices in given elections...Therefore we expect that voting participation will increase to the extent that political parties are linked with nationally identifiable cleavage groups.[15]

Thus, a simple and straightforward measure of the aggregate level of partisanship in a political system is the degree to which individuals' party preference can be predicted from a knowledge of their sociodemographic characteristics. In the specific case of Britain, the strength of this linkage is, in longitudinal terms, most comprehensively estimated by Rose's multivariate analyses of the relationship between social structure and party choice for each general election since 1959.[16] Table 2.4 documents the evolution of this relationship over the 1950 to 1983 period. The 1950, 1951 and 1955 figures are of necessity estimates and they were obtained by equating Alford's index of class voting value for 1959 with Rose's variance explained figure for the same year.[17] More specifically, this equation established that one point on the 1959 class voting index was equivalent to 0.53 per cent of the variance in party choice explained by Rose's larger set of social structural variables in the same year. Assuming a stable relationship between the two measures over the course of the preceding decade, Alford's 1950, 1951 and 1955 index values were then multiplied by this figure of 0.53 to give the estimates presented in the table. By-elections are a different matter. The linkage value prevailing at the time of any given by-election was taken to be a linear function of the change in the strength of this linkage that took place between the general elections immediately preceding and succeeding the by-election in question. Thus, if partisanship strengthens by a value of, say, plus 2 per cent and a by-election is held exactly halfway between its adjacent general elections, then the linkage estimate attributed to that by-election would be the value at the preceding general election plus 1 per cent.[18]

Table 2.4: Aggregate partisanship in the British electorate, 1950-83

	Per cent variance in party choice explained by social structure		
1950	15.3(e)[a]	1970	13.8
1951	15.8(e)	1974(F)	17.6
1955	21.0(e)	1974(O)	18.9
1959	21.0	1979	12.1
1964	19.6	1983	16.4
1966	19.2		

[a] See text for details of estimation

Until now, this measure of partisanship has been used only in cross-national studies. A potential criticism of its use in an intra-national study like this one is that, being a figure calculated over the whole of the British voting public, it does not allow for the likelihood that individual constituencies will vary in their aggregate partisanship. There is, however, good reason to believe that the difficulties raised by such variation are nowhere near severe enough to invalidate or discredit the use of the countrywide figure in Britain since a great deal of evidence exists to indicate that the level of partisanship is reasonably uniform across the whole country. While not gainsaying the differences that they themselves show to exist, Butler and Stokes, for example, observe: 'The uniformity of the relationship of class and party is far greater across the regions of Britain than it is in many countries.[19] It is certainly very similar in England and Scotland, two 'regions' that otherwise show marked discrepancies in electoral behaviour.[20] The assumption of a reasonable approximation between national and constituency levels of partisanship does not, therefore, seem unwarranted. To be sure, the imposition of a national measure of partisanship on individual

constituencies may be regrettable for the element of distortion that
it inevitably introduces into the analysis, but Britain's relative
homogeneity makes it an expediency that is tolerable and certainly
preferable to abandoning this strand of the analysis.

Having made these observations on the measurement of
partisanship in the aggregate, a few comments remain to be made
about Table 2.4. In the first place, it is noticeable from it that
partisanship declines relatively secularly when compared to voting
turnout (see Table 2.2). In other words, partisanship may be a
determinant of turnout, but it would appear to be only one of
several, hence they do not move strictly in tandem. Indeed, the
simple correlation of the two variables over our population of
constituencies is only 0.12 for general elections and 0.17 for by-
elections. Strikingly similar to the pattern of voting turnout,
however, is partisanship's relatively sharp and sustained decline
after the 1966 general election. In the six elections from 1950 to 1966
inclusive, the mean level of partisanship is 18.6 per cent, whereas it
dips four percentage points to 14.6 per cent in the remaining five
elections. This similarity indicates that the sharp decline in social
class' electoral impact from the 1970 general election onwards has
clear implications for parliamentary election turnout patterns as
well as for the erosion of the Conservative and Labour parties'
electoral hegemony.[21]

The second category of long-term determinant comprises forces
that are best conceptualised as being specific to Britain and the
folklore relating to electoral participation suggests two candidates
for inclusion in it. The first concerns the different seasons in which
parliamentary elections are held and the second differences in the
support base of the individual parties. A third candidate is the inter-
nation differences identified earlier in this chapter. The effect of
these potential determinants can be expected to manifest itself along
three dimensions: i) in general election turnout; ii) in by-election
turnout; and iii) in turnout change from general to by-election.
Moreover, if they are to be considered genuine long-term
determinants, two criteria should be satisfied. The first is that the
difference in turnout on the three dimensions should be of
substantial magnitude and the second that the differences should be
directionally uniform across the three dimensions. In other words, if
it is argued that autumn weather depresses turnout in general
elections. then the same argument can only be expected to be made
for by-elections.

To take the question of seasonal variation first, a common

argument holds that turnout levels are affected by the time of the year in which parliamentary elections are held.[22]These arguments can contradict each other, however. One view, for example, is that turnout will be low in Summer elections since many electors will be out of the country on holiday. Equally, winter weather is often argued to depress turnout since electors not only find it more difficult to get to the polls, especially if they do not have their own transport, but also they are less likely to drag themselves away from the warmth and comfort of their living rooms. To test the hypothesis of seasonal variation, Table 2.5 compares turnout patterns in elections held in Autumn and Winter on the one hand with those held in the relatively clement seasons of Spring and Summer on the other. It was not possible to keep the four seasons separate because the small number of general elections held over the 1950-83 period would have meant too few cases in the Summer and Winter categories especially.[23]

Table 2.5: Season, party and country as sources of variation in percentage voting turnout

	General elections	By-elections	Rate of change
Season			
Autumn/Winter	74.5	62.5	14.2
Spring/Summer	77.5	59.9	15.2
Incumbent party			
Conservative	76.9	61.1	15.1
Labour	74.5	60.6	14.5
Country			
England	75.8	59.9	15.8
Scotland/Wales	76.8	67.4	09.4

Immediately apparent from Table 2.5 is that the seasonal timing of parliamentary elections has no consistent effect on their turnout patterns. With a difference of 3.0 per cent, general elections show the biggest disparity between the proportion of electors actually going to the polls in Autumn and Winter on the one hand and Spring and Summer on the other. The substantive importance of this difference is undermined straight away, however, by the fact that its direction is not only reversed for by-elections, but also, at

2.6 per cent, its magnitude is almost as great as it is for general elections. In short, there is little evidence to sustain the argument that the election season variable should be treated as a long-term determinant of voting turnout.

This same conclusion holds for much the same reasons in the case of the hypothesis of an inter-party difference in turnout patterns. The source of this hypothesis lies in the class basis of the support for the British Conservative and Labour parties and the basic argument is that since people with middle class characteristics tend both to go to the polls more and to vote Conservative more, turnout can be expected to be higher in Conservative-held seats than in Labour-held ones. That is, both general and by-election turnout should be higher and the rate of change between them lower in Conservative constituencies. The evidence presented in Table 2.5 shows there to be little empirical support for this hypothesis, however. To be sure, the level of turnout in both types of election is higher in Conservative seats, but it is substantially so only in general elections. Moreover, and contrary to expectations, the drop in turnout is actually greater in this same group of seats. For want of convincing and consistent evidence, therefore, the hypothesis of inter-party differences must, like its seasonal counterpart, be rejected and the idea of conceptualising this variable as a long-term influence on electoral participation abandoned.

Exactly the opposite conclusion follows from a comparison of turnout variations across the constituent nations of Great Britain. Scotland and Wales combined show higher levels of turnout than England in both general and and by-elections, as well as a lower rate of decline between them.[24] Not only are these differences directionally consistent, i.e., all three show a relatively 'poor' performance from England, but also their magnitude is substantial on two of the three turnout dimensions; the exception being general election turnout. In at least one respect, the English turnout performance is surprising and it is that Scotland and Wales both score *lower* on a range of socioeconomic indicators that are usually associated with high turnout. Moreover, even though it has narrowed somewhat, this discrepancy has persisted over the time period covered by this analysis. A good example is the standard indicator of socioeconomic development, *per capita* Gross Domestic Product. As a proportion of the United Kingdom average and in constant 1976 figures, England scored 103 in 1966 and 102 in 1976; the same figures for Scotland are 89 and 97 respectively and for Wales 86 and 90.[25]

If the Scottish and Welsh electorate's greater politicisation cannot be explained by socioeconomic factors, it seems reasonable to look to political factors. One plausible explanation is that Scotland and Wales both have a more radical political culture and tradition than England. There is certainly plentiful evidence, both historical and contemporary, that at least one of the necessary ingredients for such radicalism is present in both peoples. This ingredient is a sense of being systematically disadvantaged by the political *status quo*. A good proportion of both peoples (72 per cent in Scotland and 46 per cent in Wales), for example, feel that their country is not as well off as the rest of Britain. Moreover, the proportion holding this view increases progressively from Conservative to Labour to nationalist party supporters.[26] Nor is this pattern of support likely to be coincidental. This sense of deprivation almost certainly helps to explain why reformist parties have long been disproportionately strong in Scotland and Wales. Both are traditional Labour strongholds and separatist nationalist parties have made unprecedented gains in both countries in recent years. Thus, the greater propensity of their peoples to make use of their ballot is probably one of the consequences of the greater political radicalism to be found in Britain's Celtic fringe.

No matter how adequate this particular explanation, however, it remains the case that the distinctiveness of Scottish and Welsh turnout patterns should, along with partisanship, be recognised as a long-term influence on British electoral politics. Having been identified, these two variables will function as control variables in each of the next three chapter's analysis of how political parties structure turnout patterns in the short term.

Notes

[1]Quoted in R.L. Leonard, *Elections in Britain* (London: Van Nostrand, 1968), p. 5. For a thorough discussion of the adequacy of this quotation, see R.K. Alderman and J.A. Cross, 'The Prime Minister and the Decision to Dissolve', *Parliamentary Affairs*, 28 (1975), 386-404.

[2]Leonard, *Elections in Britain*, pp. 119-26.

[3]David Butler and Donald Stokes, *Political Change in Britain*, 2nd ed., (London: Macmillan, 1974), pp. 172-80.

[4]These two by-elections are excluded essentially because of the abnormal pattern of party competition that characterised either the by-election itself or the preceding general election. The Bristol, South-East contest took place in August 1963 against the background of Anthony Wedgewood Benn's efforts to renounce the peerage he had inherited some three years earlier so that he could keep the Commons seat that he had won in a 1950 by-election. Upon being disqualified from the Commons for having succeeded to the peerage, Benn contested and won the resultant by-election. He was not able to take up the seat, but his Conservative opponent promised to vacate it if a subsequent change in the law permitted Benn to be reelected. The Peerage Act of 1963 introduced this change. The Conservative stood down and Benn won the by-election overwhelmingly since he had no Conservative opponent. The second contest to be excluded is Southampton, Itchen and it is unsuitable for inclusion because, prior to the by-election of May 1971, it had been the Speaker's seat and, in consequence, had not been contested by the other major party, the Conservatives, in either the 1966 or 1970 general elections. The only other by-election not to have been contested by one or other of the two major parties in this period is the Carmarthen one of February 1957. The Conservatives failed to put a candidate, but this was a practice of long standing in this constituency and thus not attributable to extraordinary circumstances. For this reason, the by-election is kept in the population.

[5]Colin Mellors, *The British M.P.: A Socioeconomic Study of the House of Commons* (London: Saxon House, 1978), pp. 27-37. More detailed reasons for the falling number of by-elections are given in David Butler, 'By-Elections and their Interpretation' in Chris Cook and John Ramsden, eds., *By-Elections in British Politics* (London: Macmillan, 1973), pp. 2-4.

[6]See, for example, David McKie, 'By-Elections in the Wilson Government' in Cook and Ramsden, eds, *By-Elections in British Politics*, 223-63.

[7]Surprisingly little has been written on British by-elections and the literature that does exist tends to be preoccupied with the phenomenon of the vote swing against the government. See Anthony King, 'Why All Governments Lose By-Elections', *New Society*, 21 March 1968, 413-15; Anthony Mughan, 'Towards a Political Explanation of Government Vote

Losses in Midterm By-Elections', *American Political Science Review*, 80 (1986); Stephanie Stray and Mick Silver, 'Do By-Elections Demonstrate a Governments's Unpopularity?', *Parliamentary Affairs*, 33 (1980), 264-70; *idem*, 'The Measurement of Change in the Popularity of Governments in United Kingdom By-Elections', *Political Methodology*, 8 (1982), 93-106; and *idem*, 'Government Popularity, By-Elections and Cycles', *Parliamentary Affairs*, 36 (1983), 49-55.

[8]The formula commonly used to adjust for the register's age can be found in Richard Rose, 'Britain: Simple Abstractions and Complex Realities' in *idem*, ed., *Electoral Behavior: A Comparative Handbook* (New York: Free Press, 1974), p. 494.

[9]A.J. Allen, *The English Voter* (London: English Universities Press, 1964), p. 11.

[10]Evidence that might be taken to support this argument can be found in Donald Stokes, 'Parties and the Nationalization of Electoral Forces' in W.N. Chambers and W.D. Burnham, eds, *The American Party Systems: Stages of Political Development* (Oxford: Oxford University Press, 1967), 182-202. This 'nationalisation' argument does not apply equally to both types of parliamentary election, however. Butler draws attention to its limitations in the context of party choice when he observes: 'However, it is plain that in general elections, national behaviour is remarkably uniform: in elections since 1950 three constituencies out of four have shown a swing within 2 per cent of the national average. In by-elections the variation has been appreciably greater.' See Butler, 'By-Elections and their Interpretation', p. 7.

[11]A simpler measure of turnout variation would be the range, i.e., the difference between the highest and lowest constituency turnouts. It is inappropriate here, however, since the range of the inter-election turnout scores is substantially smaller than that for either the general or by-election scores. But their relative smallness is in fact an artefact of comparing a longitudinal measure with a cross-sectional one. The advantage of the coefficient of variation is that it overcomes this problem by controlling for differences in the absolute size of the mean value of the three dimensions of turnout by dividing each's standard deviation by its mean. See Hubert M. Blalock, Jr., *Social Statistics*, 2nd ed., (New York: McGraw Hill, 1972), p. 88.

[12]These correlations are calculated over the 242 cases whose boundaries remained unchanged between the general elections immediately preceding and succeeding the individual by-election contests.

[13]The fifteen constituencies in which by-election turnout exceeded that in the general election are in chronological order: Carmarthen (28/2/57), Devon, Torrington (27/3/58), Argyll (12/6/58), Aberdeenshire, East (20/11/58), Kirkcudbrightshire and Wigtownshire, Galloway (9/4/59), Montgomeryshire (15/5/62), Kinross and Perthshire, West (7/11/63), Rhonnda, West (9/3/67), Lanarkshire, Hamilton (2/11/67), Ayrshire,

South (19/3/70), Merthyr Tydfil (4/5/72), Berwick-Upon-Tweed (8/11/73), Grimsby (28/4/77), Glasgow, Hillhead (27/5/82) and Darlington (24/3/83).

[14]Mitchell himself strongly denies the validity of this explanation in the case of the Grimsby by-election. See Austin Mitchell, 'The Local Campaign, 1977-79' in Robert M. Worcester and Martin Harrop, eds, *Political Communications* (London: Allen & Unwin, 1982), p. 38. A more general treatment of the whole question of candidate effect is to be found in Chapter 4 of this book.

[15]Both the quotation and the idea of measuring partisanship in this way come from G. Bingham Powell, Jr., 'Voting Turnout in Thirty Democracies: Partisan, Legal, and Socio-Economic Influences' in Richard Rose, ed., *Electoral Participation* (London: Sage, 1980), pp. 13-14. See also Powell's, *Contemporary Democracies* (Cambridge, Mass.: Harvard University Press, 1983).

[16]The 1959-83 figures are taken from Richard Rose and Ian McAllister, *Voters Begin to Choose: From Closed-Class to open Elections in Britain* (London: Sage, 1986), p. 92. A similar set of estimates of this linkage can be found in Mark N. Franklin, 'How the Decline of Class Voting Opened the Way for Radical Change in British Politics', *British Journal of Political Science*, 14 (1984), p. 484. But these are not considered as an alternative measure of partisanship since they begin only in 1964, which means that to use them would necessitate resorting to Alford-based linkage estimates for almost half the 1950-83 period and for 167, or 57 per cent, of the 294 by-election cases. A second alternative measure of aggregate partisanship is the incidence of party identification in the electorate, as reported in the various academic voting surveys from the 1964 election onwards. This measure, however, is unacceptable for the same reason as is Franklin's. It also has the additional problem that, being social pyschological in nature, it cannot be directly equated with Alford's sociological class voting index to obtain partisanship estimates for the 1950s.

[17]The values for the index of class voting are to be found in Robert R. Alford, *Party and Society: Class and Voting in the Anglo-American Democracies* (Chicago: Rand McNally, 1963), p. 103.

[18]The precise formula used in this calculation is:

$$BEP = VE1 + ((VE2\text{-}VE1)\frac{tb}{t}), \text{ where}$$

VE1=percentage of variance explained in preceding general election, *VE2*=percentage of variance explained in succeeding general election, *tb*=total number of days between the by-election and the preceding general election, *t*=total number of days between the general elections immediately preceding and succeeding the by-election.

[19]Butler and Stokes, *Political Change in Britain*, p. 128.

[20]See William L. Miller, *The End of British Politics?* (Oxford: The

Clarendon Press, 1981), pp. 140-44.

[21] On the decline of class voting, see Mark N. Franklin and Anthony Mughan, 'The Decline of Class Voting in Britain: Problems of Analysis and Interpretation', *American Political Science Review*, 72 (1978), 523-34 and Jonathan Kelley, Ian McAllister and Anthony Mughan, 'The Decline of Class Revisited: Class and Party in England, 1964-79', *American Political Science Review*, 79 (1985), 719-37.

[22] See Alderman and Cross, 'The Prime Minister and the Decision to Dissolve', p. 388.

[23] Following the *Encyclopaedia Britannica*, the seasons are defined as follows: Winter (22 December to 20 March), Spring (21 March to 21 June), Summer (22 June to 22 September) and Autumn (23 September to 21 December). This definition means that two general elections have fallen in Winter since 1950 (1950 and February 1974), five in Spring (1955, 1966, 1970, 1979 and 1983), none in Summer and four in Autumn (1951, 1959, 1964 and October 1974). With regard to general election turnout, Table 2.5 excludes six constituencies that only came into existence in the preceding general election since no party could be conceived of as holding the seat when that election was called. All were created between the 1945 and 1950 elections and they are Brighouse and Spenborough; Bristol, South-East; Dunbartonshire, East; Glasgow, Scotstoun; Leicester, North-East and Sheffield, Neepsend. Excluded from the by-election figures are Carmarthen (28/2/57) and Montgomeryshire (15/5/62) since both were held by the Liberal party when the by-election was called.

[24] There are two reasons for collapsing Scotland and Wales into a single category in Table 2.5. The first is their common disproportionate support for the Labour party and the second is that the fusion was made necessary by the need to produce a respectable number of seats in the 'non-English' categories. Had Scotland and Wales been kept separate, the fifteen by-elections that have taken place in Wales since 1950 would seem to constitute too small a number for reliable analysis, especially when boundary changes mean that three of them (Abertillery, 30/11/50; Newport, 6/7/56; and Carmarthen, 28/2/57) will automatically be excluded from the multivariate analyses undertaken in the next three chapters (see Appendix A).

[25] These figures are taken from Richard Rose and Ian McAllister, *United Kingdom Facts* (London: Macmillan, 1982), p. 156.

[26] See Anthony Mughan and Ian McAllister, 'The Mobilization of the Ethnic Vote: A Thesis with some Scottish and Welsh Evidence', *Ethnic and Racial Studies*, 4 (1981), p. 195. A similar, longer term view can be found in Michael Hechter, *Internal Colonialism: The Celtic Fringe in British National Development, 1536-1966* (London: Routledge and Kegan Paul, 1975.

Introduction

The basic assumption guiding the next three chapters is that voting turnout varies so markedly across British constituencies even when elections occur in them simultaneously that some part of this variation must be accountable for by the purposive efforts of political parties to influence voting turnout patterns to their own electoral advantage. In constituencies where by-elections have taken place since 1950, for example, the range of general election turnout stretches from 52.6 per cent at one extreme to 87.2 per cent at the other. The same figures for by-elections are even further apart at 24.9 and 85.1 per cent respectively and the rate of change of turnout from general to by-elections is similarly vast, stretching from an increase of 11.4 per cent to a decline of 39.4 per cent.[1]

To recap, the forces responsible for this variation have been argued to be of two types, long-term and short-term. In the specific context of Great Britain, the long-term political influences on electoral participation have been identified to be partisanship and country. Short-term influences, in contrast, will be more numerous and diverse in their identity since the potential for influence resides in a range of them stretching from purposive party activity in the form of, say, canvassing or nominating experienced and attractive candidates to less predictable phenomena that are simply beyond the manipulative skills of even the best organised political party - the weather on election day, for instance. If only because of the existence of such phenomena, this analysis cannot aspire to provide anything like a comprehensive explanation of turnout patterns. Its more modest aim is to explore how political parties shape this aspect of the voting act.

In this regard, Britain's political parties are best viewed not as unitary, hierarchical organisations, but as agencies whose potential for influence exists on two largely independent levels, the local and the national. In overall terms, this analysis devotes more attention to the local, or constituency, level since it is the constituency party that is the moving force in parliamentary elections, owing its preeminence to the performance of two crucial functions that common sense would suggest have a direct bearing on patterns of electoral participation. These functions are the nomination of a candidate to contest the seat under the party's flag and the conduct and co-ordination of this same candidate's campaign in the constituency. In theory, the local party is subject to national party oversight, and even intervention, in its performance of both these functions, but the practice is for it to retain its autonomy under all but the most exceptional circumstances. Thus, any influence that the national party may have on constituency turnout patterns will be taken to make itself felt directly through the perhaps unwitting medium of its own popularity and standing with the electorate rather than through its direct orchestration of electioneering activity in the constituency.

Three aspects of party influence constitute the substantive foci of the next three chapters. This one, Chapter 3, deals with the relationship between the party-defined political context of the election and voting turnout. Chapter 4 examines the effects of the personal and political characteristics of the candidates nominated by the parties to contest the seat and Chapter 5 repeats this exercise for the standing in national public opinion of the parties and their leaders. This chapter ordering might seem a little perverse at first since it does not follow the chronological sequence of the electoral process itself. The nomination of candidates obviously precedes the contesting of the election, whereas these two stages of the electoral process are treated the other way round herein. The adoption of this particular format rests on the assumption that candidates are chosen less on the basis of their personal characteristics and more on that of the political context of the constituency they are seeking to represent in Parliament. For this reason, the context plays an important, and logically prior, role in the determination of who gets selected. More pragmatically, it might also be noted that, the substantive chapters being treated as separate entities, it makes little or no practical difference in which order they are presented.

The Political Context

Broadly speaking, the term 'political context' refers to the immediate political conditions and circumstances surrounding an election and impinging on its outcome. Apart from the long-term forces of country and partisanship, this context comprises two analytically distinct dimensions, the 'local' and the 'national'. The former encompasses those characteristics peculiar to the individual electoral unit, in this case the parliamentary constituency. The latter, on the other hand, comprises those chacteristics that transcend the territorial boundaries of this unit and relate to the parties as nationwide institutions. This distinction is at its most obvious in the comparison of general elections and by-elections. The former are truly national in the sense that they are characterised by the election of a parliamentary representative in all of a country's constituencies simultaneously; the entire country is placed on an election footing for the period of the campaign. By-elections, in contrast, are purely local affairs in that they involve the choice of an MP in perhaps no more than a single constituency at a time; they are consequently more likely to slip by unnoticed or to be more readily discounted by electors as being of little moment and therefore not worth the effort of voting in. This is the distinction that lies at the root of the contrast between them as high- and low-stimulus elections respectively. The very scale of general elections means that, relative to by-elections, public interest, awareness and involvement in them is likely to be high, party loyalties awakened and strong and turnout consequently to be high.[2]

National party leaders do, however, have the potential to enhance the stimulus level of by-elections by a variety of means, including in particular the ability to determine their precise timing. This ability comprises three decisional components and these will serve as three of the four measures of national political context. The first component is the determination of when the election will be held. This decision is certainly a matter of some consequence for the inter-party distribution of the by-election vote since research has shown that British governments in fact pass through a three-phase cycle in their electoral fortunes. 'After the election of a government there is a "honeymoon" period when the level of expectations derived from the party's election promises are not expected to be fulfilled immediately...as the government moves into its middle years, expectations are still unfulfilled, and the government's performance becomes unacceptable to its supporters, who switch votes or abstain. As the election approaches...the voter "homes" on his "normal" party.'[3]

If this kind of systematic abstention there really is, then by-election turnout levels can be expected to follow the same cyclical pattern as government vote losses. To test this hypothesis, the honeymoon phase has been defined as lasting for six months after

Table 3.1: The by-election turnout cycle

Phase of cycle	Honeymoon	Middle	Homing
Per cent turnout	63.1	61.1	64.5
No. of cases	(15)	(199)	(26)

the general election and the homing phase for six months prior to the next one. Experimentation with a number of different time periods showed this to be only one allowing for both variation across the categories in Table 3.1 and a respectable number of cases in each of them. In other words, it is the pattern of turnout itself that dictates the temporal delimitation of the phases in the life cycle of governments. Table 3.1 presents the evidence for a turnout cycle in British by-elections. There does seem to be one, but insofar as the category means are not very different, it is not strongly defined. Nonetheless, there is sufficient variation across them to warrant the inclusion of a timing variable in this investigation of the determinants of turnout. It is a dummy variable scored '1' for by-elections that take place within six months of either the preceding or succeeding general election and '0' for those that do not.

It is worth noting briefly here that an attempt to introduce a similar timing variable for general elections failed. In an effort to determine whether turnout in them varied with a government's length of time in office, the effect of a 'months in office' variable was investigated. Unfortunately, however, it proved to be highly inter-correlated with two other, more substantively important independent variables, the level of partisanship (a zero-order correlation of 0.88) and the size of the governing party's parliamentary majority (a zero-order correlation of 0.84). The variable had, therefore, to be discarded.

The second component of the party leadership's timing decision relates to the visibility, or saliency, of elections. This is hardly a pertinent consideration in the case of general elections since these embroil the whole country and are, in consequence, necessarily highly salient. By-elections are potentially another story, however. Occurring sporadically in perhaps no more than one of over six hundred constituencies, they are less likely to attract serious and sustained coverage by the national media in particular so that public awareness of them will probably suffer. This is a particularly important consideration in a country like Britain where the popular media in all its forms is predominantly national in organisation and orientation. By-election turnout is thus likely to suffer for want of public awareness and interest. Confronted with this relative apathy, the major parties have actually sought to bring home to the public the national importance of by-elections by establishing the practice of holding a group of them on a single day in preference to holding them singly as vacancies arise. 'Over the years the Whips have changed their habits and, in conjunction with party headquarters, have given more importance to timing, and to national as opposed to local considerations...In the 1960s...there was much more of a tendency, whatever the delay involved, to group (by-elections) together...'[4]

If the effect of grouping by-elections is indeed to increase their stimulus level and to make the public more aware of their national importance, then the larger the number of them held simultaneously, the higher should be the level of voting turnout in them. Hence, the second national context variable included in this chapter is the number of by-elections held on the same day. As it transpires, their number actually varies between one and six and, on the occasion that six of them took place simultaneously, the rate of change of turnout was far from uniform, ranging from a drop of 12.3 per cent to one of 28.3 per cent.[5] This observation further vindicates the argument that by-election turnout merits consideration in its own right since its barely understood dynamic would appear not to be governed by national forces alone.

The final component of the timing decision involves the electoral register. This is the official document that determines who will receive a ballot paper at election time and it is compiled every October to come into effect the following February. It is 16 months old, therefore, before it is taken out of circulation and replaced. During this period, people on the register inevitably die, change address or move out of the constituency altogether so that, as it ages, the register becomes an increasingly inaccurate representation of the eligible electorate in the constituency. This inaccuracy, it has been argued, can be manipulated to partisan advantage: 'It is highly unlikely that a Labour Prime Minister would hold an election near the expiry of an old register, since the Labour party normally suffers from a stale register. The Conservative party is either indifferent or might, with its better organisation for mobilising postal votes for the electors who have moved constituencies since the register was compiled, see a tactical advantage over Labour in an out-of-date register.'[6] Scored in months, the age of the register is an independent variable in this chapter's analysis.

The fourth measure of national political context is 'parliamentary marginality' and it refers to the absolute size of the governing party's overall majority in the House of Commons. For by-elections, it is the majority prevailing when the by-election is called and for general elections it is that prevailing when Parliament is dissolved in preparation for an election. It stands to reason that, especially in a nationalised polity like Britain, the parliamentary distribution of seats could quite easily have some direct bearing on turnout patterns in the constituencies. In this regard, it should be borne in mind that three post-war elections, 1950, 1964 and October 1974, have returned governments with small and barely workable parliamentary majorities and another, February 1974, even returned a minority government. Under such circumstances, all political parties can be expected to be especially keen to get their supporters to the polls, particularly in by-elections since their outcome is generally less predictable. The governing party will be anxious to retain the seats it already holds in face of the very real and ever-present potential for their loss; it will also want to do well simply to bolster its public image and the party's internal morale. The opposition parties, on the other hand, will be at least as keen to undermine the government's credibility, to improve their own and perhaps even to precipitate a premature general election while the party in office is weak and on the defensive. For these reasons, it would seem reasonable to expect that turnout will be high when parliamentary majorities are small.[7]

The concept of parliamentary marginality nicely bridges the gap between the national and local political context since the constituency characteristic that is best known for its positive effect on voting turnout is marginality of a different kind. This is constituency marginality and it can be operationally defined in two ways. The more common of them relates to the inter-party distribution of the vote in individual elections and its measure is the winning margin enjoyed by the victorious party over its second-placed rival in the preceding parliamentary election. The second measure is both more demanding and less flexible in the short-term since it defines a marginal constituency as one that has changed party hands one or more times over a specified period of time, usually the last several elections. Hereinafter, the former will be termed electoral marginality and the latter a marginal, as opposed to safe, seat. Since it is the more common, electoral marginality will be dealt with first.

When defined in terms of the winning margin of votes, there can be no doubt that marginality is empirically associated with the level of voting turnout in the subsequent parliamentary election; the simple correlation between the two in this group of by-election constituencies is highly significant at 0.32 for general elections and 0.30 for by-elections. What these coefficients signify is the smaller the difference in the vote shares of the first- and second-placed parties in an election at time t, the higher is the turnout at election $t+1$. Negatively signed coefficients are avoided by subtracting the difference in the vote shares of the first two parties from 100 per cent so that the larger the remainder, the more marginal the constituency. While affecting the character of the relationship not at all, this transformation has the distinct advantage of generating coefficients that, being positively signed, can be interpreted more intuitively as indicating that marginality increases turnout levels.

Again an aspect of the local political context, there is a second kind of constituency marginality and it has its basis in the distinction between safe and marginal seats. Two constituencies might well have the same narrow margin of victory in an election, but one of them could have changed hands in the recent past and the other not. If this were the case, the parties in the volatile seat would in all likelihood put in a more intense electioneering effort than the simple margin of victory would predict. To allow for this situation, this analysis includes a measure of constituency marginality that is defined in terms of the safeness of the seat. If it has changed party hands in any one or more of the previous three parliamentary elections, it is placed in the marginal category and scored '1'. If, on the other hand, it has remained under the control of the same party over this same three-election period, it is classified as safe and scored '0'.[8]

The final aspect of the local political context is the number of parties fielding a candidate in the election. Whether or not a party puts up a candidate is clearly an important dimension of its electioneering politics and the importance of the candidate number variable has already been established in aggregate studies of general election turnout; it gets higher as the number of candidates increases.[9]No elaborate justification of the inclusion of this variable need, therefore, be presented here. The mean number of general and by-election candidates between 1950 and 1983 is given in Table 3.2. Immediately noticeable is that there are no separate entries for the

Table 3.2: Mean number of candidates in general and by-elections by Parliament

	1950-55	1955-59	1959-64	1964-66	1966-70	1970-74	1974-79	1979-83
	General elections							
Candidates	2.2	2.3	2.4	2.9	2.7	2.9	3.5	5.1
	By-elections							
Candidates	2.4	2.8	3.7	3.8	3.8	4.2	5.8	7.8
No. of cases	(43)	(31)	(60)	(13)	(37)	(10)	(29)	(17)

1950-51 and February-October 1974 Parliaments.[10]This is because once those constituencies with changing boundaries have been excluded, there is only one by-election in each of them and these are included in the 1951-55 and October 1974-79 categories respectively. Over this period, the minimum number of general election candidates in any one constituency was two and the maximum six. At two and sixteen, the equivalent figures for by-elections show a far wider range; they also reflect a wider diversity of candidates. In addition to those from the established parties, they include, amongst others, candidates intent simply on drawing attention to themselves - army personnel standing in order to bring their military service to a premature end or persons giving voice to genuine local or personal issues or grievances through their campaign, for example. Whatever their precise reason for standing, however, Table 3.2 shows that the number of candidates has been increasing steadily over the whole period in by-elections and since the 1970s especially in general elections. In both instances, the growth in their number is partly a function of the deterioration in the Conservative and Labour parties' hold on the loyalty of the electorate in the 1970s and partly a function of the election deposit not keeping up with the rate of inflation and therefore acting as less of a deterrent to 'crank' candidates. This deposit was set at £150 in 1948 and has remained at this figure throughout the period of this analysis.

Level of Turnout

The preceding section, then, has identified the short-term, political contextual characteristics that might be expected to complement long-term forces in affecting turnout patterns in British parliamentary elections. To summarise them for the sake of easy reference, the local contextual characteristics are electoral marginality, the safeness of the seat and the number of candidates contesting the election. Their national-level counterparts are parliamentary marginality, the age of the register on which the election is fought, the timing of the election and the number of by-elections held on the same day. It should be remembered, however, that these last two variables are applicable only to by-election contests and are not included at all in the general election regression analyses. Thus, when the long-term forces of country and partisanship are also taken into account, there are nine independent variables in the full by-election equation and seven in the general election one.

The statistical technique used to ascertain the effect on turnout patterns of the individual long- and short-term forces is the stepwise variant of ordinary least squares regression analysis, which assumes that variables are, to a reasonable approximation, linear and additive. It is also the analytical technique used in subsequent chapters. The tables in the text comprise the parenthesised zero-order correlation coefficients to the left of the variable names and the matching standardised regression coefficients, or beta weights, to the right of them. The latter are preferred to their unstandardised counterparts because they convey the relative importance of independent variables within equations. In other words, the constituent betas of each equation can be directly compared so as to assess their explanatory importance relative to each other.[11] Not all the independent variables will always figure in each equation and this is because their appearance requires the satisfaction of the inclusion criterion that their partial regression coefficent have a value at least twice the size of their standard error. This statistical criterion of substantive importance is used to help avoid the articulation of conclusions founded on tenuous relationships. Missing data are rarely a problem in this data set. When present, however, they are treated by the pairwise present procedure, which is statistically preferable to the usual alternatives.[12]

The result of regressing general and by-election turnout levels on the gamut of contextual variables for all constituencies is presented in Table 3.3 and its immediately striking feature is is marginality's clear explanatory pre-eminence in both types of election. The only other variable common to both outcomes is the long-term one of country and it signifies that apparent differences of political culture and tradition ensure that voting turnout is generally lower in England than it is in Scotland and Wales, especially in by-elections. The vexing feature of this table, though, is the substantive interpretation of marginality rather than country. Nor can this issue be avoided since this variable repeatedly figures as a prominent, and very frequently the most powerful, predictor of turnout patterns. But prediction is not explanation, so some detailed consideration must now be given as to how its effect is best interpreted in substantive terms.

Essentially, marginality is a measure of the competitiveness of a constituency and there exists considerable evidence, from both without and within this analysis, to suggest that it can be taken as a surrogate measure of the organisational mobilisation of support undertaken by political parties especially, but also by organisations affiliated to them and other interested partisan and non-partisan groups and individuals. Research on the United States, for example, indicates quite clearly that party organisation and strength are intimately related to the degree of partisan competition in the individual states.[13] In the same vein, a comprehensive study of the marginality and turnout relationship in British general elections between 1959 and 1970 concludes: 'Higher turnout in marginal seats is rarely the product of a "rational" appreciation of the situation by voters, but results from parties creating greater awareness amongst voters or simply cajoling them into going to the polls'.[14] This same study also demonstrates that a more direct measure of party mobilisation, campaign expenditure, explains only slightly more variation in general election turnout than does marginality.[15] The final seal of approval for this interpretation of marginality's influence comes from the non-academic source of journalistic observation of electioneering politics 'on the ground'. 'There may well be narrow margins dividing those in the first three places. The Conservative majority here (Glasgow, Woodside) in 1959 was 2,084 and the three major parties are not sparing themselves to ensure that in the next fortnight there will be famous men to plead and loyal workers to canvass'.[16]

The second batch of evidence in favour of this interpretation of marginality's effect comes from within this analysis. It might be

Table 3.3: Standardised coefficients for the regression of turnout on the political context variables by type of election

General election turnout			By-election turnout		
(.32)	Marginality	0.31	(.30)	Marginality	0.32
(-.30)	Candidates	-0.24	(.23)	Country	0.28
(.07)	Country	0.15	(.21)	Partisanship	0.18
(.21)	Parliamentary marginality	0.13		R^2=20.0	
	R^2=22.4				

argued that, being in large part determined by the immediate political circumstances of particular elections, the organisational mobilisation of voting support is a dynamic and adaptable phenomenon, whereas marginality somehow seems to be a relatively static constituency characteristic that changes little over short periods of time. Thus, this argument would conclude, how can one of these phenomena be expected to act as a valid surrogate for the other? This argument is mistaken, however. The truth of the matter is that electoral marginality is anything but a static phenomenon; its simple correlation with itself in adjacent general elections is no more than 0.73 and by-election marginality is correlated with that in the preceding general election at a value of only 0.48.[17].

A second demanding test of the marginality's validity as a measure of voter mobilisation involves its relationship to turnout in adjacent elections. If it is indeed a surrogate for organisational effort, which is itself adaptable to short-term changes in the political circumstances of individual constituencies, then turnout in a particular election should be more highly correlated with the closeness of that same election than with the closeness of its immediate predecessor. This is because the mobilisation effort will be dictated more by expectations of the outcome of the forthcoming election than by knowledge of the outcome of its predecessor. And such proves indeed to be the case. The zero-order correlation of by-election turnout with by-election marginality is 0.47, whereas its correlation with the marginality of the preceding general election is substantially lower at 0.30. The equivalent figures for general election turnout are 0.34 for marginality in the same general election and 0.32 for its predecessor.[18] This smaller difference between the two coefficients in the case of general elections should not be taken to negate the overall argument since it is a difference that is only to be expected. After all, general elections are high-stimulus in character, which, means that the party-led organisational mobilisation of the vote is is only one of several powerful stimuli getting voters to the polls. By-elections, on the other hand, are low-stimulus contests in which organisational effort should be an especially effective influence on turnout patterns precisely because it meets with comparatively little competition.

To return to Table 3.3 after this lengthy digression, once the common importance of marginality and country is noted the similarities between the two regression outcomes end. By-election turnout is the more easily interpreted since, electoral marginality apart, short-term forces, be they local or national, play no role in structuring it. The long-term forces of country and partisanship, on the other hand, do influence it and they come to the explanatory fore precisely because by-election turnout as a whole is unresponsive to its immediate political context. It is misleading, therefore, to distinguish by-elections from general elections in terms of their turnout dynamic being more heavily influenced by local considerations. The more accurate characterisation of them is that, taking place in a contextual vacuum, this dynamic is almost as little influenced by local as it is by national forces. Only tradition and force of habit complement the competitiveness of the seat in fuelling by-election turnout.

It is apparent from even the most superficial glance that this contextual vacuum does not afflict general election turnout to the same extent. Again, marginality is its primary predictor, but the ostensibly local contextual variable of candidate number ranks second and the national one of parliamentary marginality third. More unexpectedly, though, the influence of both these last-named variables is in the opposite direction to that which was anticipated, candidate number proving to be negative in its effect and parliamentary marginality positive. Since these two variables remain prominent and directionally consistent in their influence throughout this chapter, these anomalous findings cannot be ignored. The easiest way around the interpretational problem they present would be to seek to dismiss their effect as some kind of statistical artefact, but, as will become apparent presently, it is a problem that occurs too frequently and too consistently for this explanation to be very persuasive. The better strategy is to reconceptualise the two variables. To take parliamentary marginality first, that a large majority in the House of Commons stimulates general election turnout rather than depresses it suggests that this variable is, in fact, some kind of indicator of residual government popularity on completion of its term of office. Thus, it would seem that the the greater any government's initial popularity, the higher its popularity will remain over the course of its term in power despite the disillusionment that will almost inevitably encourage some of its supporters to stay away from the polls. This hypothesis will be given further support when turnout levels in government and opposition seats is compared a little later in this chapter.

Table 3.4: Number of candidates by mean turnout in general elections

Number of candidates	2	3	4	5	6
Per cent turnout	62.2	61.1	62.6	52.2	46.8
No. of cases	(112)	(96)	(27)	(4)	(1)

The explanation of candidate number's negative effect appears a little more intractable since it has been claimed elsewhere that the presence of Liberal and nationalist candidates serves to increase general election turnout and not to depress it.[19] The quickest way to unravel this puzzle is to examine the bivariate relationship and Table 3.4 indicates that there is in fact no clear, linear relationship between general election turnout and candidate number in any but the small number of constituencies with four or more aspirants to the House of Commons. That there is nonetheless a strong negative relationship overall may mean that the candidate number variable is acting as a surrogate for some other, 'hidden' variable. The most likely such variable would seem to be a constituency characteristic, like urban decay, that is itself associated with low turnout and some idea of its identity would seem to be best gained through an examination firstly of the constituencies boasting four or more candidates and secondly of the parties, other than the Conservatives, Labour and Liberals, presenting candidates in these constituencies. The two pieces of information might then intermesh to provide some insight into what it is about these constituencies that attracts candidates from the minor parties in question.

The problem is not so easily resolved, however, since the constituencies in question appear to have little, if anything, in common beyond the number of candidates attracted to their general election contest.[20]As might be expected, the 'extra' candidates come most commonly from the Scottish and Welsh nationalist parties and the National Front. More precisely, eleven of the thirty-two contests included a nationalist candidate and another twelve one from the National Front. But these constituencies appear to be very different in terms of their sociodemographic characteristics. Nationalist candidates, for example, are as likely to be found in highly rural constituencies like Carmarthen in Wales and Roxburghshire, Selkirkshire and Peebleshire in Scotland as in heavily industrialised ones like Rhonnda, West and Glasgow, Queen's Park. Similarly, the National Front puts up candidates in constituencies as unalike as the inner city Manchester, Central and the seaside resorts of Bournemouth and Southend. Thus, there appear to be no good grounds for arguing that the candidate numbers variable is 'fronting' for some constituency characteristic whose effect is not directly controlled for in Table 2.3.

What the thirty-two contests do have in common, though, is their timing. None of them took place before the 1964 general election and only four of them occurred before the one in 1970. Moreover, Liberal party general election candidatures follow the same pattern; the party fought only 61 of this analysis' 184 (33.2 per cent) by-election constituencies before 1970 and 48 of the 56 of them (85.7 per cent) afterwards. In other words, the increase in general election candidatures coincides more or less fully with both the period of partisan dealignment in the British electorate and the decline in what was earlier called institutionalised turnout in general elections (see Table 2.1). To put it simply, minor party candidates became more common because the long-hegemonic major parties had become electorally vulnerable. Thus, this aggregate variable is probably best interpreted as signalling a generalised loss of confidence in, and disillusion with, the Conservative and Labour parties, a development that has discouraged some electors from going to the polls in the first place and has made those who do go more volatile in their voting habits in the second.[21]

Granting this interpretation, the general election candidate number variable is better counted as a national electoral force rather than as a local one. This issue does not come up with regard to by-election turnout since, there, the candidate number variable enjoys no explanatory importance. Seeing Table 3.3 in this light, a more coherent and 'national' interpretation of general election turnout suggests itself. Organisational mobilisation remains the principal explanatory variable, but it is a less monoplistic short-term force than it is for by-elections since a second substantial influence is an erosion of public confidence in Britain's governing parties and a third is the lasting popularity of the outgoing government. Thus, the manipulation of turnout levels can be seen to be less under party control in general elections because of the role played by relatively immutable national forces in their turnout dynamic.

In sum, then, the aggregate perspective presented in Table 3.3 is instructive for both its confirmation of the pre-eminence of the local consideration of the competitiveness of the seat in explaining variation in constituency turnout levels in both types of parliamentary election and its indication that, beyond this commonality, the two have little in common. In broad terms, by-election turnout is unaffected by the remaining short-term forces, even the local ones and, in their absence, habit and tradition, as represented by the long-term forces of country and partisanship, emerge to explanatory importance. Turnout in general elections, in contrast, is more responsive to the national dimension of its overall political context.

But, as interesting as this general picture may be, it is far from the total insight that can be gained into the relationship between political context and turnout levels. Following upon the demonstrated importance of marginality, a good, *prima facie* case can be made for the argument that at least this dimension of elections' overall political context can be expected to have a differential effect in Conservative- and Labour-held seats. This argument has its basis in the differential quality of the two parties' organisation at the national and local levels and its thrust is that the Conservative party's is far superior. This is in part because of its greater resources and its ability to raise money more easily, but also, and more importantly, because of the contrast in its attitude to the whole question of organisational efficiency and its desirability:

> How do we explain the apparently endemic difference in the quality of Labour and Conservative organisation in this country?...(O)ne explanation is that the Labour party lacks an instinct for public relations; it's a party which by the very nature of its composition doesn't rate the smooth running of an operation very highly. I'm sceptical of this explanation. For one thing, the Labour party does in fact contain a large number of people who do possess managerial skills, or at least who ought to do so in view of their job or their education. In any case, the European experience

does show that, now and historically, it is the working-class parties which are the best organised... So one has to find the explanation somewhere else. I would suggest that it has to do with the radical temperament in British politics to which a part of the Labour party is heir. This temperament is distrusful of paternalism, distrustful of efficiency for efficiency's sake, distrustful of the mechanisation of any aspect of human life but particularly of government and the formation of public opinion.[22]

To compound the Labour party's problems, this traditional distrust of efficiency has been compounded in recent years by a marked decline in its membership and organisation at the local level. Starting from a baseline of over 1,000,000 in the early 1950s, the party has been losing fee-paying members at an average rate of more than 11,000 per year.[23]Its national organisation has deteriorated as well. The number of full-time agents in its employ, for example, has dropped from 296 in 1951 to 52 in 1983. In this same year of 1983, the Conservative party employed 320 full-time agents.[24]

When all these factors are taken together, the Labour party can only be expected to be less successful than the Conservative party in mobilising support at election time. In other words, other things being equal, marginality should be less effective relative to other determinants of turnout in Labour seats than it is in Conservative ones. To test this hypothesis, the population of constituencies was divided into Conservative- and Labour-held seats at the time of the general and by-election and the level of turnout in each of them then regressed on the gamut of political context variables.

Before considering the outcome of this exercise, however, a word of caution is in order. The hypothesis of greater Conservative effectiveness cannot, of course, be directly tested herein since it is impossible to obtain separate, constituency-based measures of organisational activity for the two parties and their allies. But while regrettable, this is not a fatal problem since this particular analysis' aim is not to test directly the hypothesis that the two parties differ in their effectiveness in getting out the vote. Rather, its aim is necessarily the more modest one of demonstrating the constituency characteristic of party incumbency mediates and 'distorts' the basic relationship between turnout and political context displayed in Table 3.3. The precise role of party organisation in this process is undoubtedly interesting and probably considerable, but its actual contribution cannot be estimated here. Without constituency-based electioneering data by party, the precise reason(s) for the effect, if any, of party incumbency must remain in the realm of inference and speculation. All that this analysis does is to test the hypothesis of its importance, while fully recognising that, unlikely as it may be, any relationship that does emerge could well be due to factors other than organisational disparities between the incumbent parties.

Table 3.5: Standardised coefficients for the regression of turnout on the political context variables by Conservative and Labour incumbency and type of election

General election turnout					
Conservative incumbency				*Labour incumbency*	
(.49)	Marginality	0.53	(-.39)	Candidates	-0.39
(-.14)	Candidates	-0.16	(.19)	Country	0.28
	R^2=27.6		(.20)	Marginality	0.22
				R^2=24.6	

By-election turnout					
Conservative incumbency				*Labour incumbency*	
(.26)	Marginality	0.29	(.32)	Marginality	0.37
	Parliamentary		(.26)	Country	0.34
(.29)	marginality	0.25		R^2=21.3	
(.30)	Partisanship	0.24			
	R^2=20.1				

Bearing this proviso in mind, the effect of Conservative and Labour incumbency is summarised in Table 3.5, which has two salient features. The first, and most immediately relevant, is its convincing demonstration that the identity of the party holding the seat has a profound influence on marginality's importance in stimulating turnout. This variable may be the principal predictor of both general and by-election turnout in Conservative seats, but it enjoys this position only in by-elections when it comes to Labour seats. Of course, if it is organisational effort that is responsible for the incumbency effect, the contrast between the two groups of seats could be due either to differing levels of effectiveness given similarly developed organisations or simply to differing levels of organisational development. Without an independent measure of such development, though, it is impossible to choose between these two explanations. Suffice it to note simply that the evidence suggests that voter mobilisation is not as successfully undertaken in Labour-held seats, but it is not really important to determine why since to do so would not alter the basic conclusion that the competitiveness of a seat is a less effective general election turnout stimulant in those constituencies where Labour is the incumbent party.

Table 3.5's second, and closely related, salient feature is its confirmation of a systematic, if less marked, difference between general and by-elections as well as between Conservative and Labour seats. The essence of this difference is that, in contrast to general elections, marginality is the single best predictor of turnout in both groups of seats in by-elections. Perhaps reflecting the Conservative party's clear organisational supremacy in general elections especially, marginality is the overwhelming dominant predictor in seats where this party is incumbent, whereas it is a poor third in Labour seats. Thus, even a close contest is less successful in offsetting public disillusion's negative effect on general election turnout levels in Labour-held seats than it is in Conservative ones. This same disparity does not affect by-election turnout, however; marginality is the strongest influence in both groups of seats. The most likely explanation of this inter-election difference again relates to organisation. The effect on turnout of Labour's organisational disadvantage can be expected to be especially obvious in general elections since these require it to stretch its relatively limited electioneering resources over the whole country. In by-elections, its disadvantage should not have the same effect since it can concentrate these resources in the one or small number of constituencies being fought. More generally, this lesser ability to get out its general election vote might help to explain why Labour's share of the electorate has fallen more sharply than the Conservative's despite dealignment from both of them.[25]

There can be no doubt, then, that the identity of the party incumbent in the constituency substantially mediates the political context's overall effect on the level of turnout, in general elections especially. Another variable that might well exercise a similar mediating influence relates less to the constituency and more to the national political setting and it is whether the seat is held by the government or opposition party. The rationale underlying this hypothesis is the interpretation of election outcomes as being in large part a retrospective judgment on the performance of the party in office.[26] If such is indeed the case, then the incumbent government's popularity, as measured by its parliamentary majority, should positively influence turnout levels even after the effects of the other contextual variables have been controlled.

Table 3.6: Standardised coefficients for the regression of turnout on political context variables by government and opposition incumbency and type of election

	General election turnout					
	Government incumbency				*Opposition incumbency*	
(.37)	Marginality	0.32		(.23)	Marginality	0.30
(-.35)	Candidates	-0.30		(-.17)	Candidates	-0.23
	Parliamentary				$R^2=10.4$	
(.31)	marginality	0.22				
(.07)	Country	0.18				
	$R^2=29.8$					

	By-election turnout					
	Government incumbency				*Opposition incumbency*	
(.26)	Marginality	0.29		(.38)	Marginality	0.37
(.24)	Country	0.26		(.19)	Country	0.25
	Parliamentary			(.23)	Partisanship	0.22
(.27)	marginality	0.24		(.20)	Timing	0.18
	$R^2=20.0$				$R^2=28.1$	

Table 3.6 proves there to be mixed support for this hypothesis. On the credit side, the government's popularity can be seen to boost both general and by-election turnout in the seats that it holds, but it has no effect in opposition seats. The government simply does not seem to be a significant reference point in either type of election in this latter group of seats.

But the more interesting feature of Table 3.6 is the general one that government or opposition incumbency is not as strong and distorting an influence as is Conservative or Labour incumbency. That is, the regression outcomes in Table 3.6 are more like those for the population of constituencies as a whole, especially insofar as marginality is the foremost predictor in all four of them (see Table 3.3). In Table 3.5, in contrast, this variable enjoys a similarly uniform pre-eminence in Conservative, but not Labour, seats. What this means is that the 'national' consideration of government or opposition incumbency does not have the same implications for turnout levels as the 'local' one of Conservative or Labour incumbency. Such a difference can only strengthen the conclusion of a significant local component in the turnout dynamic of both general and by-elections. Of course, it would be misleading to overstate this similarity since the two types of election are also consistently and clearly differentiated by the relative contribution of the national political context to their turnout dynamic, a difference that is most obviously highlighted by the explanatory prominence of the candidate number (public disillusion) variable in general elections and its total absence in by-elections (see Tables 3.5 and 3.6). Nonetheless, the strength of localism, even if unevenly distributed across the two types of parliamentary election, should caution against overdeterministic generalisations that declare electoral behaviour in Britain to be a function essentially of *post hoc* reactions to government performance.

To summarise, then, three conclusions, one very specific and two relatively general, follow from the analysis up to this point. The first is that turnout in both general and by-elections is responsive primarily to the short-term force of the organisational mobilisation of voter support in the constituency. The long-term forces of partisanship and country, and especially the latter, also play an explanatory role, but it is relatively secondary and sporadic. The second conclusion is that general and by-election turnout dynamics are affected differently by the short-term contextual forces. The candidate number variable figures in all the general election equations and in none of the by-election ones. Parliamentary marginality, on the other hand, figures in some general and some by-election equations, although only in Conservative or government seats. Thus, in general, national forces relating to declining public confidence in the traditional parties of government, as well as to more immediate government popularity, intervene more to structure the level of general election turnout. Their failure to play a similar role in by-elections leaves a vacuum that tends to be filled by the relatively passive long-term forces of country and partisanship. Turnout in this type of election is consistently influenced by marginality alone among the short-term forces and the relative unimportance of either its national or local political context imparts to it an introverted character. This observation preempts to some extent the final conclusion, which is that turnout's association with the political context of parliamentary elections is mediated more by the local factor of Conservative or Labour incumbency and less by the national one of government or opposition incumbency. Moreover, the likely explanation of the importance of the Conservative as against Labour incumbency distinction relates to organisational disparities between the two parties at both the national and local levels. At least as it relates to turnout levels, then, the national character of British electoral politics can very easily be overstated.

Rate of Change of Turnout

Having noted the importance of the local factors of the closeness of the contest and party incumbency in explaining turnout levels, attention now switches to the explanation of the rate of change of turnout from general to by-elections. Averaging out at 14.6 per cent and with a coefficient of variation of 0.63, inter-election change is clearly more variable than either cross-sectional general or by-election turnout, which have coefficients of variation of 0.09 and 0.18 respectively. What is more, it is a dimension of change that would appear to be particularly susceptible to short-term forces, not least because the drop in turnout reverses itself almost wholly in the general election succeeding a series of by-elections. Thus, between 1950 and 1983, the mean decline of 14.6 per cent becomes a mean increase of 12.6 per cent when pendulum swings the other way and change is measured from the by-election to the succeeding general election. Given the decline in institutionalised turnout over this same period, this figure of 12.6 per cent represents to all intents and purposes a reassertion of the *status quo ante*.[27]

The study of inter-election turnout change is not quite as straightforward as it might first seem, however. The first problem lies in the specification of the factors, or types of factor, that can be expected to influence it. One category that immediately suggests itself is matching change in the political context variables, or at least in those of them where change is a meaningful concept. The identity of the country in which elections take place, for example, will not change from general to by-election. But others of them can and do. Thus, if partisanship, for instance, stimulates turnout, then the weaker it becomes from one election to another, the bigger should be the drop in turnout between them. But the magnitude of turnout change will also be determined to some degree by the political context of the by-election itself. That is, if the by-election involves a marginal seat, mobilisational effort should ensure that, other things being equal, the decline in turnout is not as great as it would have been were the seat safe. Similarly, the higher the level of partisanship in the electorate at the time of the by-election, the smaller should be the magnitude of the drop in turnout relative to the preceding general election.

A complete analysis of the dynamics of turnout change, therefore, will include both cross-sectional and change variables, which is what this one does. That is, to the contextual variables that figure in the earlier by-election turnout analysis are now added variables measuring inter-election change on the following: partisanship, electoral marginality and parliamentary marginality. A slight technical problem is that the two versions of the candidate number variable on the one hand and of the electoral register variable on the other are intercorrelated at values of -0.93 and -0.83 respectively. To avoid a severe collinearity problem, the cross-sectional versions of both these variables are excluded from further consideration. It was decided to retain their change versions because of this section of the chapter's primary concern with the effect on the rate of change of turnout of corresponding change in the independent variables.[28]

A second methodological point concerns the measurement of change in the dependent and independent variables. To take the dependent variable first, to calculate the rate of change of turnout simply by subtracting the level of by-election turnout from that in the preceding general election encounters a problem of equivalence. A suburban constituency, for example, may have a turnout of 80 per cent in the general election and 60 per cent in the subsequent by-election, whereas the same figures for an inner city seat whose social and economic characteristics mean that its turnout level is habitually lower might be 40 and 20 per cent. But despite being of the same percentage value, is the decline in turnout really of equivalent magnitude in these two seats or, under these circumstances, is it not wiser to control for the factors making for perenially lower turnout in the second constituency by calculating change in proportionate rather than absolute terms? The analysis in the remainder of this book is based on the proportionate estimate of change, which is measured by subtracting by-election from general election turnout and dividing the difference by the same general election figure. Instead of a common 20 per cent, this measurement strategy gives the more realistic change measures of -25 and -50 per cent respectively for the above two constituencies.[29]

The measurement of change in the independent variables is less problematic from both a conceptual and methodological viewpoint. These are measures the magnitude of whose variation in the short term is precisely what is of interest. In varying, they are not constrained in the long term from moving freely upwards or downwards so there is no need to standardise them by calculating them as a proportion of some base figure. Such standardisation might well be advisable when, for example, two countries are compared and one's party system is founded on a much higher level of partisanship in the electorate than the other. It is not necessary in a single-country study like this one, however. The simple subtraction of the by-election from general election score, therefore, is an adequate measure of change on the independent variables.

Table 3.7: Standardised coefficients for the regression of turnout change on the political context variables[*]

Inter-election turnout change

(-.36)	Δ Marginality	-0.52
(-.17)	Marginality	-0.41
(-.25)	Country	-0.24
(.16)	Δ Partisanship	0.23
(-.22)	Δ Candidates	-0.16
(-.02)	Partisanship	-0.12
(-.10)	Timing	-0.11
	$R^2 = 39.4$	

[*] Δ denotes change

Having made these methodological clarifications, we can now turn to the question of what variables influence the rate of change of turnout between general and by-elections. Table 3.7 summarises the regression of turnout change on the gamut of cross-sectional and change independent variables and its outstanding feature is the unquestioned primacy of electoral marginality. The victorious party's winning majority averaging out at 12.4 per cent in by-elections and 14.6 per cent in the preceding general election in the same constituency, by-elections are on the whole more competitive than general elections. Thus, the more competitive the general election contest and, still more importantly, the more competitive the seat becomes in the by-election, the lower the drop in turnout between the two elections. Importantly, though, seats do not become more competitive of their own accord, so to speak. Since only a relatively short space of time separates them from general elections, it is not as if, for example, the socioeconomic character of constituencies can change to favour one or other party less. Equally, there is no reason to believe that there will be any great change in the electorate's disposition towards the individual parties between the two elections. Special circumstances may promote such change in specific instances, but not across the board. Rather, by-elections are more competitive largely because parties contesting them make them so. The departure of the incumbent candidate contributes to the contest's becoming more open than for some time and this inspires the competing parties to especially great efforts to get their supporters to the polls. The result is that the drop in turnout that almost inevitably accompanies the transition from high- to low-stimulus elections is significantly reduced.

The second, and related, noteworthy feature of Table 3.7 is its demonstration that the turnout change dynamic is more akin to its by-election than to its general election counterpart. This can be seen in the top three variables being the same, and in the same rank order, as they are for cross-sectional by-election turnout (see Table 3.3).[30] The similarity should not be overdrawn, however. In the first place, the turnout change dynamic is more sensitive to the effect of its short-term political context, as is indicated by the simple fact that, marginality apart, no contextual variables figure in the cross-sectional by-election equation, whereas there are two of them (change in the number of candidates and the timing of the by-election) in Table 3.7. Second, turnout change is more responsive to local forces than is by-election turnout and this is manifested in two ways in Table 3.7. The marginality variables dominate the equation more clearly than for by-election turnout and the candidate number variable figures in the turnout change equation but not in the by-election turnout one. Nor can the local character of the turnout change dynamic be diluted by the argument that the change version of the candidate number variable should, like its cross-sectional counterpart, be interpreted as a national force. If it were so, its relationship to turnout decline would be positive since the increase in public disillusion (as measured by the growth in the number of candidates) would be expected to make turnout fall even further. As it is, however, the relationship is negative, which means that the appearance in a number of by-election contests of parties that had not fought the preceding general election attenuates turnout decline. The very fact that such appearances are selective indicates that changing candidate numbers is properly interpreted as a constituency-specific effect.

All in all, therefore, the explanation of turnout change has a local character that makes it as different from by-election turnout as is general election turnout with its more markedly national dynamic.

Table 3.8: Standardised coefficients for the regression of turnout change on the political context variables by Conservative and Labour incumbency and type of election[*]

	Inter-election turnout change					
	Conservative incumbency				*Labour incumbency*	
(-.41)	Δ Marginality	-0.67		(-.34)	Δ Marginality	-0.54
	Δ Parliamentary			(-.21)	Marginality	-0.51
(.07)	marginality	0.33		(-.22)	Country	-0.27
(-.09)	Marginality	-0.31		(-.19)	Timing	-0.18
(.10)	Δ Partisanship	0.23			$R^2 = 40.5$	
(-.24)	Country	-0.13				
	$R^2 = 38.5$					

[*] Δ denotes change

Given this conclusion, it is not surprising that, as with by-election turnout, the identity of the party incumbent in the constituency introduces an element of distortion into the overall relationship depicted in Table 3.7. If anything, though, the extent of this distortion is greater for turnout change. To be sure, Table 3.8 shows that the seat's becoming more competitive in the by-election remains by far the most potent contextual influence in both Conservative and Labour-held seats. But beyond this commonality, the two groups of seats have little in common.

For a start, the relationship is considerably stronger relative to the other variables in Conservative seats; these seats may become competitive at the same rate as Labour ones, but the turnout effect of this trend is greater in Conservative seats. Given this party's superior organisation overall, a plausible explanation of this discrepancy is that it is simply more efficient at discouraging by-election abstention among its own supporters, especially when the seat is at risk. It might be said to 'outmobilise' Labour in this regard. The aggregate patterns of turnout and voting change certainly lend support to this interpretation of the different strength of the relationship in the two sets of seats. Conservative seats just do not become as marginal in by-elections as do Labour ones; the gap separating the first two parties shrinks by 1.9 percentage points in the former and 2.5 points in the latter. In addition, the Conservative party also maintains its vote share more successfully in its own seats than does Labour in seats where it is incumbent; the Conservative vote drops by 5.2 percentage points, whereas Labour's falls by 6.9 per cent.

In the second place, the table suggests that an additional explanatory factor is that electorates in Conservative seats are more sensitive and responsive to their immediate political environment. On the one hand, their abstention is more likely as governments have become unpopular enough to lose seats in previous by-election contests. On the other hand, the partisan context of the by-election affects their voting turnout; the weaker this becomes, the more likely their abstention becomes. It might well be, of course, that both these developments are more likely to encourage organisational apathy at by-election time than they are to elicit a direct response from attentive constituency electorates. But in view of middle class' more widely shared sense of class self-interest, as reflected in its relative cohesiveness as a voting bloc, some part of their effect at least will reflect the greater sensitivity to current political developments of predominantly middle class Conservative constituency electorates.[31]It would appear that this class is more vigilant in the sense that when it feels its interests to be under threat, it more readily takes to the polls to protect them. Such vigilance being absent in Labour constituency electorates, their rate of change of turnout is structured by the relatively passive forces of the country in which the by-election takes place and its timing.

Table 3.9 shows that whether the by-election seat is held by the government or opposition party also distorts, and each in its own way, the overall turnout dynamic. The effect of changing marginality is of roughly similar magnitude in both seat groupings, but they have little else in common. Unlike in either Conservative, Labour or government seats, neither the long-term forces of country and partisanship nor short-term contextual forces other than marginality influence the rate of change of turnout in opposition seats. It is as if so little is at stake in these seats and so little attention is paid to them that by-elections in them become utterly introverted events which are oblivious to their short-term political context, probably because they do not excite their electorates. After

Table 3.9: Standardised coefficients for the regression of turnout change on the political context variables by government and opposition incumbency and type of election[*]

		Inter-election turnout change			

	Government incumbency			*Opposition incumbency*		
(-.29)	Δ Marginality	-0.41		(-.30)	Δ Marginality	-0.50
(-.06)	Marginality	-0.35		(-.36)	Marginality	-0.46
(-.30)	Country	-0.28			R^2=31.8	
(.31)	Δ Partisanship	0.28				
(-.26)	Δ Candidates	-0.21				
	R^2=33.1					

[*] Δ denotes change

all, if the by-election does not offer the opportunity to pass judgment on the government of the day's performance, why bother even to vote if one is not mobilised by long-standing and deeply felt party loyalties or by the campaigning efforts of local party organisations? Not surprisingly given this argument, by-elections in government seats are not equally impervious to the influence of either long-term forces or their short-term political context. In addition to the marginality variables, country, partisanship and an increase in the number of candidates all influence the rate of change of turnout in them. Moreover, these last two variables are both cause and consequence of the anti-government reaction common in by-elections. On the one hand, governments through their policies and actions help to determine the partisan context of elections and declining partisanship, in weakening party loyalty, makes it easier for supporters to abstain from voting if dissatisfied with their party's performance in office. On the other hand, minor party candidates are more likely to stand in by-elections when the party in power is vulnerable and their presence gives disgruntled government supporters the opportunity to vent their dissatisfaction without having to abstain. Whichever of these scenarios prevails, government supporters fail to turn out and it loses votes.[32]

But, importantly, if weakening partisanship and the presence of minor party candidates do facilitate a vote swing against the government, they do so only in the seats it holds. As with cross-sectional turnout, there is no evidence of a structuring effect for the growth of anti-government sentiment in opposition seats. The government is would appear not to be a salient reference point where direst action 'to throw the rascals out' is not possible.

Conclusion

The most general conclusion to be drawn from this chapter is that the short-term political context of parliamentary elections has a profound effect on their turnout patterns and this effect is independent of the long-term forces of partisanship and country. More specifically, the contextual variable with the greatest impact of all on both the level and rate of change of turnout is the organisational mobilisation of the vote. Electoral marginality may be a somewhat crude measure of this phenomenon, but there is no reason to believe that it is not a valid one. Certainly, the relationship consistently takes the form that would be expected given the ample evidence of the Conservative party's superior electoral organisation at both the local and national levels. It is difficult to see, therefore, how at least some considerable part of this variable's impact cannot be the product of the short-term effort undertaken by the major political parties and their collaborators to influence the election outcome to their own advantage. It cannot be doubted, however, that controlling for marginality, whatever its precise meaning, makes any other short-term relationships that do emerge all the more credible and convincing.

In designating such mobilisation a local force, it is recognised that national party leaders and organisations do themselves contribute to the mobilisation of support through activities like the provision of campaign funds and of prominent party leaders to visit the constituency in order to sustain the morale of party activists and to mobilise the 'faithful'. Such national activities, however, are at the behest of, and tailored to the needs and circumstances of, the individual constituency parties. It is, after all, the local party organisations that are responsible not only for the nomination of candidates, but also for the conduct of their campaign. Thus, since ultimately it is filtered through the agency of the local party, what influence the national party organisation may have on constituency turnout patterns can only be subordinate and indirect.

Once attention switches to short-term forces other than

marginality, the picture becomes more complicated since their effect is more variable across both turnout dimensions and type of seat. Broad, internally coherent and consistent patterns do emerge from this complexity, though. Most saliently, by-election turnout is all but totally impervious to their influence; it is as if this type of election takes place in a contextual void where tradition and habit, as represented by the long-term forces of country and partisanship, alone complement marginality in structuring the level of turnout. Since marginality enjoys much the same prominence in the explanation of general election turnout, it would seem misleading to represent by-elections as having an inveterately more local character than general elections. This is especially so since the one short-term force to have an effect more than once on by-election turnout is the national one of parliamentary marginality. General election turnout and inter-election turnout change, on the other hand, are more susceptible to short-term party influence, even if this influence is not uniform across seat groupings. Generally speaking, electorates in Conservative and government seats are more affected by short-term forces than are those in Labour and opposition ones.

Moreover, not only are the general election and turnout change dynamics more susceptible to short-term forces, but also these forces are distinctive in character. Being public disillusion and parliamentary marginality for general elections and the by-election appearance of minor party candidate(s) for turnout change, the forces comprising their respective dynamics can, broadly speaking, be labelled 'national' and 'local'. Buttressing the validity of this distinction is that the local consideration of electoral marginality is always preeminent in the explanation of turnout change, but not always so in that of general election turnout. Public disillusion is the strongest predictor of this turnout dimension in Labour seats and comes a close second in government ones. In turnout terms at least, therefore, the 'local' counterpart to the 'national' general election is less the by-election itself and more the change between general and by-election.

In conclusion, the evidence denies the existence of a uniform, nationwide dynamic structuring either the level or rate of change of turnout in British parliamentary elections. Thus, the argument that a homogeneous political culture and tradition means that the moving forces in British electoral politics are national in origin and electoral consequence is as misleading as it is oversimplified. The truth of the matter is that whether they emanate from the long-term differences in political culture and tradition between Britain's constituent nations or from short-term constituency differences in the organisational mobilisation of support, sub-national forces fundamentally shape the dynamics of voting turnout in both general and by-elections. To be sure, the extent of their contribution may vary according to turnout dimension and type of seat. Nonetheless, our understanding of the sources of stasis and change in turnout patterns would be the poorer if the recognition of such complexity were sacrificed to an interpretation of British electoral politics that ignored the substantial contribution of sub-national forces.

Notes

[1] These turnout figures are calculated over the 240 cases whose boundaries remained unchanged between the first and second general elections preceding the by-election. This stipulation for inclusion was necessitated by the use of marginality in the preceding general election as an independent variable in the analysis of general election turnout. It should also be noted that all the data analysis in the remainder of this book is carried out over these same 240 cases in order to make the substantive findings of Chapters 3, 4 and 5 comparable. The omission of the 54 cases with changing boundaries makes little or no difference to the results obtained, however. It will be remembered from Chapter 2, for example, that, over the full complement of 294 cases, the coefficient of variation for general election turnout is 0.09, for by-election turnout it is 0.19 and for inter-election turnout change it is 0.63. These same figures for the 240 cases are 0.09, 0.18 and 0.63 respectively.

[2] The distinction between 'high-' and 'low-stimulus' elections in the British context is expounded in Anthony King, 'Why All Governments Lose By-Elections', *New Society*, 21 March 1968, 413-15. A fuller statement of this general thesis is Angus Campbell, 'Surge and Decline: A Study of Electoral Change' in Angus Campbell, Philip E. Converse, Warren E. Miller and Donald E. Stokes, *Elections and the Political Order* (New York: Wiley, 1966), 40-62.

[3] Stan Taylor and Clive Payne, 'Features of Electoral Behaviour at By-Elections' in Chris Cook and John Ramsden, eds, *By-Elections in British Politics* (London: Macmillan, 1973), p. 345.

[4] David Butler, 'By-Elections and their Interpretation' in Cook and Ramsden, eds, *By-Elections in British Politics*, p. 4.

[5] Only once have as many as six by-elections been held simultaneously. The day was 16 November 1960 and the constituencies involved were: Bolton, East; Mid-Bedfordshire; Devon, Tiverton; Hampshire, Petersfield; Shropshire, Ludlow and Surrey, Carshalton. Their respective general and by-election turnouts were: 80.9 and 68.2 per cent; 84.5 and 71.1 per cent; 80.7 and 68.4 per cent; 73.6 and 53.6 per cent; 76.2 and 63.6 per cent and 82.5 and 54.2 per cent.

[6] R.K. Alderman and J.A. Cross, 'The Prime Minister and the Decision to Dissolve', *Parliamentary Affairs*, 28 (1975), p. 388.

[7] The measure of parliamentary marginality is the number by which the governing party's seats in the House of Commons exceeds the combined total accruing to the other parties in the Chamber. No account is taken of the Speaker's party affiliation or of the number of seats waiting to be filled through the device of the by-election. This is because such subtleties are likely to escape the public at large. Instead, even the most informed elector is unlikely to know anything beyond the government's working majority at the time of the by-election. The parliamentary consequences of a particular

by-election are then likely to be assessed, if at all, against this touchstone. Equally, local parties are likely to be 'driven' more at election time by the broad distribution of seats than by their precise division.

[8]A more sensitive measure of the safeness of a seat would have been the number of times it had changed hands in the last three elections. The number actually changing hands, however, was so small that a simple dummy variable was thought to be the more reliable measure. For instance, only 38 seats switched party control one or more times in the three parliamentary elections preceding each by-election and only 9 did so in the immediately preceding general election.

[9]See for example, Michael Steed, 'The Results Analysed' in David Butler and Michael Pinto-Duschinsky, *The British General Election of 1970* (London: Macmillan, 1971), pp. 387-89.

[10]In point of fact, there were fourteen by-elections in the 1950-51 Parliament, but only one of constituencies, Birmingham, Handsworth, was either not newly created for the 1950 election or had not experienced a boundary change prior to it. In contrast, there was only one by-election in the very short February 1974-October 1974 Parliament.

[11]A good overview of the regression model is Fred N. Kerlinger and Elazar J. Pedhazur, *Multiple Regression in Behavioral Research* (New York: Holt, Rinehart & Winston, 1973). To limit the problem of multicollinearity, a tolerance level of 50 per cent was specified in the regression runs. In other words, an independent variable is not allowed to enter the regression equation if 50 per cent or more of its variance can be explained by the independent variables already in the regression equation.

[12]See Bradley R. Hertel, 'Minimizing Error Variance Introduced by Missing Data Routines in Survey Analysis', *Sociological Methods and Research*, 4 (1976), 459-75.

[13]Samuel C. Patterson and Gregory A. Caldeira, 'The Etiology of Partisan Competition', *American Political Science Review*, 78 (1984), 691-707.

[14]D.T. Denver and H.T.G. Hands, 'Marginality and Turnout in British General Elections', *British Journal of Political Science*, 4 (1974), p. 35. For the same thesis in regard to local elections, see P. Fletcher, 'An Explanation of Variations in "Turnout" in Local Elections', *Political Studies*, 17 (1969), 495-502. The hypothesis that close elections encourage individual 'rationality' has been similarly dismissed for American presidential elections. See Carroll B. Foster, 'The Performance of Rational Voter Models in Recent Presidential Elections', *American Political Science Review*, 78 (1984), 678-90.

[15]Denver and Hands, 'Marginality and Turnout', pp. 32-34.

[16]See *The Times*, 7 November 1962, p. 7.

[17]It is interesting to note in passing that changing turnout patterns are an important reason for marginality's surprisingly low correlation with itself from general to by-elections. The simple correlation between the drop

in turnout and the drop in marginality is 0.39

[18]Despite being more strongly correlated with turnout, this chapter does not use the marginality of the election itself as an explanatory variable. Instead, it retains the marginality of its predecessor for two reasons. Firstly, change in the level of marginality is later used as an independent variable in the explanation of inter-election turnout change. Secondly, the effect of the marginality of the election itself may to some extent be confounded with that of other variables, like candidate quality, which are of interest in their own right.

[19]Steed, 'The Results Analysed', pp. 487-89.

[20]In view of the prominence of the candidate number variable, it is worth naming the thirty-two constituencies. In the 1964-66 Parliament, there is only Roxburghshire, Selkirkshire and Peebleshire. The 1966-70 Parliament encompasses the Carmarthen, Rhonnda, West and Cambridge constituencies. In 1970-February 1974, there is Merthyr Tydfil and Dundee, East. In the October 1974-79 Parliament, there were four or more candidates in the following constituencies: Coventry, North West; Cambridge; City of London and Westminster, South; Grimsby; Bournemouth, East; Glasgow, Garscadden; Lambeth, Central; Wycombe; Hamilton; Manchester, Moss Side; Berwick and East Lothian and Pontefract and Castleford. In the 1979-83 Parliament, the constituencies in question are: Manchester, Central; Hertfordshire, South West; Southend, East; Warrington; Crosby; Glasgow, Hillhead; Beaconsfield; Merton, Mitcham and Morden; Gower; Birmingham, Northfield; Peckham; Glasgow, Queen's Park; Bermondsey and Darlington.

[21]The phenomenon of partisan dealignment is the subject of Bo Sarlvik and Ivor Crewe, *The Decade of Dealignment* (Cambridge: Cambridge University Press, 1983). Interestingly, if this interpretation of the candidate number variable has any validity, there is a direct comparison to be drawn with the United States where attitudinal change, in the form of weakening party identification and declining confidence in governmental responsiveness, has been invoked to explain the drop in institutionalised turnout in both congressional and presidential elections in recent' years. See Paul R. Abramson and John H. Aldrich, 'The Decline of Electoral Participation in America', *American Political Science Review*, 76 (1982), 501-21.

[22]Peter Pulzer in Robert M. Worcester and Martin Harrop, eds, *Political Communications: The General Election Campaign of 1979* (London: Allen and Unwin, 1982), pp. 52-53.

[23]See especially Paul Whiteley, 'The Decline of Labour's Local Party Membership and Electoral Base, 1945-79' in Dennis Kavanagh, ed., *The Politics of the Labour Party* (London: Allen and Unwin, 1982), 111-34. A general treatment of party revenues and expenditures is Michael Pinto-Duschinsky, *British Political Finance 1830-1980* (Washington D.C.: American Enterprise Institute, 1981).

[24]The 1951 agents figure comes from Butler and Pinto-Duschinsky, *The British General Election of 1970*, p. 268. The 1983 figures are also from the Nuffield study of that year's election, David Butler and Dennis Kavanagh, *The British General Election of 1983* (London: Macmillan, 1984), p. 248. See also Pinto-Duschinsky, *British Political Finance*, p. 158. It is also worth mentioning that a consistent theme of the Nuffield studies is the Conservative party's superior organisation.

[25]Ivor Crewe, 'Great Britain' in Ivor Crewe and David Denver, eds, *Electoral Change in Western Democracies: Patterns and Sources of Electoral Volatility* (London: Croom Helm, 1985), 100-50. See also Ian McAllister and Anthony Mughan, 'Attitudes, Issues and Labour Party Decline in England, 1974-79', *Comparative Political Studies*, 18 (1985), 37-57.

[26]See, for example, Morris P. Fiorina, *Retrospective Voting in American National Elections* (New Haven: Yale University Press, 1981).

[27]The simple comparison of these mean turnout change figures is not meant to imply that the two processes are explainable by the same forces. This analysis investigates the change in turnout from general to by-election. Its neglect of the change from by-election to general election should not be interpreted to mean that the two processes are assumed to be symmetrical in this sense.

[28]It is also the case that the change versions of both variables are the more highly correlated with turnout change so that to retain them in preference to their cross-sectional counterparts means that the null hypothesis of no effect for these particular short-term forces is being put to a more rigorous test.

[29]In point of fact, it makes little difference whether the absolute or proportionate measure of turnout change is used in the analysis since their zero-order correlation is 0.98.

[30]This observation, of course, applies only to the cross-sectional version of the marginality variable since the change version is not included in the estimation of the by-election equation.

[31]See Richard Rose, 'Britain: Simple Abstractions and Complex Realities', in *idem*, ed., *Electoral Behavior: A Comparative Handbook* (New York: Free Press, 1974), 481-541.

[32]See Anthony Mughan, 'Towards a Political Explanation of Government Vote Losses in Midterm By-Elections', *American Political Science Review*, 80 (1986).

The Candidates in the Constituency and
    Turnout

Introduction

In a polity like Britain that is dominated by strong, disciplined
parties, it is easy to lose sight of the fact that the public face of
elections is less a contest between party organisations and more one
between their nominated candidates in the constituency. After all, it
is the candidate who is the contact point between the semi-secret
local party organisation and the larger electorate. Their centrality to
the electoral process notwithstanding, however, there is considerable
uncertainty as to whether the candidates in the constituency enjoy
an independently influential role in its workings. Empirical research
on this question is scarce, but the common assumption tends to be
that they do not. One traditional text on British party politics, for
example, denies them any role with the assertion that 'electors (in
Britain) vote for parties and not for candidates'.[1] This view is not
uncommon among practicing politicians either. In the words of one
MP: 'I've always viewed the candidate as being of no more than
marginal   importance,   and   I   saw   nothing   in   Grimsby   (his
constituency), neither the 1977 by-election nor the 1979 general
election, to change that view.'[2] For him, 'a by-election campaign
has powerful momentum. The candidate is just the figurehead for
the national party...A performing chimpanzee can fight a general
election...We held the seat because Grimsby was marginal...Turnout
was up, rare in a by-election, and our whole strategy had been to get
our people out, knowing they would vote for us if they voted at all.'[3]
    This opinion is strongly stated; it also emphasises that getting
its supporters out to vote looms large in any party's efforts to
improve its vote share. Party activities undertaken to this end, in
other words, also involve influencing who votes and so can be used
to justify the broad hypothesis of a turnout effect, albeit that their
ultimate goal is to affect the distribution of the vote. But is it an
opinion that is any more persuasive for being strongly stated? At a
minimum, there is good reason not to let it go unquestioned and not
the least reason is that other political activists appear to subscribe
to the opposite opinion. Local party selection committees, for

example, attach a great deal of importance to choosing the 'right' candidate for their constituency. They look on the candidate not simply as grist for an inexorable party machine, but as a valuable asset with the potential to mobilise support for the party independently of, and in addition to, this machine.[4] This is also the view of 'the national agencies of each party...(which) want their by-election candidates to be especially attractive to win whatever additional votes personal qualities can win.'[5] The grounds for assuming a candidate effect appear even stronger in the case of sitting MPs since incumbency often carries in its wake a 'personal vote', the importance of which is that it can bring non-partisan support to the polls and thereby help insulate the individual parliamentarian against the vicissitudes of his party's popular standing in the country at large.[6] Finally, local candidates have been demonstrated to have an electoral impact in other Anglo-American parliamentary democracies, including the only one of them to have a unitary political structure in common with Britain, New Zealand.[7]

In view of this uncertainty and ambiguity, it would seem both appropriate and timely to test empirically the hypothesis of a candidate effect on constituency turnout patterns. First of all, though, the range of politically relevant candidate characteristics has to be specified and their choice justified.

Candidate Characteristics

Before their electoral importance can be assessed, some attempt has to be made to specify what it is about the composite object known as a parliamentary candidate that, individually and in the aggregate, might influence whether or not electors take up their option to vote. Speaking to this question, this chapter identifies three distinct groups of candidate characteristics, or attributes, that are potentially related to constituency turnout patterns. These are: (i) the personal characteristics of candidates; (ii) their previous electioneering and political experience; and (iii) their local connections.

Personal characteristics are those attributes that inhere in the candidates themselves, attributes that were with them before entering the political world. They can range from relatively ethereal and non-visual personality traits like charisma to readily apparent and immutable ones like age and sex. But in the absence of suitable survey data, most potentially relevant characteristics lie beyond the reach of this analysis since they cannot be measured retrospectively. Nonetheless, studies of the candidate selection process have identified a number of 'objective' characteristics that appear to be held in high regard by local party selectors. Their relative importance may vary from party to party, but these characteristics are predominantly age, sex, occupation and type and level of education. These same characteristics need not be thought important in a prospective representative by non-activists, though. Indeed, there are two reasons to believe that the only personal attributes with any prospect of influencing turnout patterns are those that cannot be masked or bypassed by the candidate and so are immediately and unavoidably apparent to the elector. These are age and sex.

The first of these reasons relates to the 'maximising' election strategy usually undertaken by parliamentary aspirants. The essence of this strategy is its attempt to attract the support of as wide a range of individuals and social groups as possible and it entails the avoidance, wherever possible, of issues that set the candidates apart from any significant section of the electorate that they are cultivating. Even if they do not attempt the impossible and set out to appeal uniformly to the whole electorate, they still go out of their way to avoid alienating any significant section of it unnecessarily.[8] Thus, they would not normally boast in their campaign of their personal wealth, of having gone to public school or of having received a university education since the majority of the constituency electorate, not having shared these social advantages, could resent it. The same goes for occupation. Most parliamentary candidates are privileged in the sense of being drawn from the professions; few electors are similarly privileged. Indeed, it is only in the relatively small number of socially homogeneous communities, like mining constituencies, that a candidate might see it to be in his interest to make a campaign issue out of his socioeconomic background. In the normal run of things, caution dictates that it is a matter best left alone.

The second reason for the hypothesised importance of age and sex relates to electors' often-demonstrated limited awareness and knowledge of politics in general and of the candidates on offer to them in particular. These limitations are likely to be especially pronounced when the candidates in question are local rather than national personalities since they would attract relatively little media attention, especially from radio and television. Hence they would have even less chance of being well-known to what would by and large be a politically apathetic constituency electorate, especially in low-stimulus by-elections. The plain fact of the matter is that if they react to candidates at all other than through their habitual party loyalties, the vast majority of electors will likely be influenced by candidates' superficial characteristics rather than by what it knows of their political ideology or issue positions. For these two reasons as well as for other potentially relevant data being unavailable, then, only the personal characteristics of candidate age and sex are investigated herein.

Table 4.1: Age and sex of candidates by party and type of election

Party	General elections		By-elections	
	Sex	*Age*	*Sex*	*Age*
Conservative	.98	46.2	.95	38.6
Labour	.94	49.2	.95	40.1
Liberal	.94	40.4	.94	41.4
Nationalist	.94	42.4	.90	37.3

The mean sex and age of the individual parties' general and by-election candidates are set out in Table 4.1; the Scottish and Welsh nationalist candidates are grouped into a single category because their numbers are too small for reliable analysis when kept separate. If a candidate is female, she is scored '0' and if male '1' so that, for example, the figure of .95 for Conservative by-election candidates means that 95 per cent of the party's standard bearers between 1950 and 1983 have been male. The table itself contains few surprises. Major party general election candidates in particular tend to be older, not least because a good proportion of them will have been incumbent MPs for some years. On the other hand, although female Conservative and nationalist candidates are to be found a little more commonly in by-election contests, there is little difference in the sexual composition of the individual parties' candidatures. Parliamentary candidates are overwhelmingly male, so much so that there is no instance of a general or by-election contest in this population of constituencies in which all the candidates have been female.

The second group of characteristics to be investigated comprises the constituency candidates' prior electioneering and political experience. If 'political' is narrowly defined as experience of parliamentary office, the two sets of experiences are conceptually distinct phenomena since an individual could stand in any number of contests without ever getting elected. This fate is especially likely to befall the candidates of Britain's minor parties because of the electoral system's in-built bias in favour of the larger Conservative and Labour parties. In empirical terms, however, the two dimensions of experience prove to be virtually synonomous, largely because the great demand for parliamentary candidatures in these two parties means that unsuccessful contestants rarely get to fight more than one constituency and then they generally get no more than two chances to win it. The result is that only successful candidates manage to accumulate anything like extensive electioneering experience, and this most often in the same constituency. For this reason, the number of years that a candidate has spent as an MP is as much a measure of his electioneering experience as it is of his more general political experience.

The importance of prolonged parliamentary service to the same constituency is that it affords a variety of advantages that office-holders can turn to their own electoral benefit. Not only do they acquire substantial electioneering experience and expertise, but their incumbency also affords the opportunity to build up a personal following in the constituency. This is a commonplace notion in academic and journalistic circles and can be defined as 'that portion of a candidate's electoral support which originates in his or her personal qualities, qualifications, activities and record'.[9] The hypotheses tested in this chapter are that two important sources of such support are service to the constituency and service to the nation through the achievement of senior governmental office.

There can be little doubt that MPs are at least presented with the opportunity to feather their own electoral nests through furthering the interests of the constituency as a whole and helping individual constituents with personal problems of various kinds. 'Nursing' of this kind can be expected to boost turnout levels precisely because it is non-partisan; electors go to the polls not out of a sense of party loyalty or because they have been canvassed, but because of their personal loyalty to the incumbent MP. In this analysis, an MP's personal following will be measured by the number of years he has represented the constituency and it is labelled 'constituency MP'. Some long-serving members may, of

Table 4.2: Political experience of candidates by party and type of election

Party	General elections			By-elections		
	Years as MP	Constit. MP	Senior office	Years as MP	Constit. MP	Senior office
Conservative	7.41	6.47	1.27	0.82	0.00	0.13
Labour	7.60	6.53	1.10	0.70	0.06	0.15
Liberal	0.02	0.12	0.05	0.69	0.03	0.18
Nationalist	0.00	0.00	0.00	0.04	0.00	0.00

course, enjoy less grass-roots popularity than other, perhaps more charismatic short-serving ones, but that does not invalidate the measure. On the contrary, it means that it underestimates the personal following of the genuinely popular member.[10]

By its very nature, though, the notion of a personal following as thus defined has no meaning when applied to by-election candidates since, as Table 4.2 clearly indicates, it is extremely rare for them to have represented the seat being contested on some previous occasion.[11] By-election candidates could, however, have a roughly similar magnetic effect as a result of the kudos attaching to prior service in Parliament, even if as the elected representative of another constituency. Labelled 'years as MP', this variable will be included in the by-election regression equations.[12] Table 4.2 indicates that differences in the prior political experience of the major party candidates are small; those of the Labour party are slightly more likely to have spent more time in Parliament and to have represented the same constituency during this period, whereas Conservative MPs are a little more likely to have attained senior political office. Liberal and nationalist candidates, in contrast, have virtually no prior parliamentary experience and were it not for the 1981 creation of the Social Democratic party (SDP) by four ex-Labour senior ministers and its subsequent electoral alliance with the Liberal party, the Liberal scores in the table would be of the same order as the nationalist ones.[13]

A personal following for an MP could also be grounded in his attainment of senior governmental office. The visibility and respect that often acccrues to major politicians in their national leadership role could well lead their constituents to feel a sense of personal responsibility, rooted perhaps in some notion of serving the national interest, for their reelection. Alternatively, this same visibility could instil a sense of determination among opposition party supporters that the politician should not be reelected. Either eventuality could bring people to the polls who would otherwise have stayed at home. Moreover, the longer the MP has been a high-ranking politician, the greater should be his visibility and its effect on turnout. This hypothesis will be tested, seniority being measured by the length of time the MP has been a member of the Privy Council and thus the holder of that salient badge of political eminence, the title 'Right Honourable'. Since it is far from unknown for senior politicians to lose or resign their seat and then seek reentry to Parliament through a by-election victory, this variable will figure in the analysis of by-elections as well as of general elections.[14]

The final group of characteristics of interest concerns candidates' grass-roots connections with the constituency. The reasoning here is that, being something of a 'favourite son', such candidates could well mobilise support by exploiting these connections, which are measured by two variables. The first is a dummy based on whether or not the candidate has held elective office in a branch of local government within whose territorial jurisdiction all or part of the constituency falls; it is labelled 'local office'.[15] The second measure of a candidate's local connections is intended to measure his career commitment to a constituency and it is the proportion of all his parliamentary election contests that has been fought in that constituency. The British practise of 'carpet-bagging' candidates moving around the country in search of a preferably safe seat means that this variable should be a more sensitive measure of local connections and standing than it would be in, say, the USA where aspirants to the House of Representatives almost invariably come from the district they are contesting despite there being no legal obligation that they do so. This variable is labelled 'candidate exclusivity'.[16]

Table 4.3 raises the very real prospect of some explanatory importance for these 'local' variables. In contrast to Table 4.2, all four candidate aggregates have non-trivial scores on each of them, which suggests that they are politically important considerations for parties' candidate selection committees; they may be equally so for party supporters in the electorate. Moreover, there is for the first time an appreciable gap between Conservative and Labour scores. This gap is especially pronounced with respect to local government office where the relatively high Labour score in both general and by-elections suggests that this experience is more of a prerequisite for

Table 4.3: Local ties of candidates by party and type of election

	General elections		By-elections	
Party	Candidate exclusivity	Local office	Candidate exclusivity	Local office
Conservative	0.48	0.14	0.14	0.13
Labour	0.49	0.17	0.10	0.23
Liberal	0.69	0.16	0.51	0.13
Nationalist	0.94	0.06	0.89	0.14

career advancement there than within the Conservative party. But whether these distributional differences will have any importance when the variables' effect on turnout patterns is investigated is the concern of the next section of this chapter.

Level of Turnout

Before proceeding to the presentation and interpretation of this chapter's findings, two observations directly relevant to this exercise are in order. The first one is substantive and concerns the 'proper' conceptualisation of the conglomerate candidate characteristics variable. It goes almost without saying that its relationship to turnout can, and should, be examined for the individual parties, Conservative, Labour, Liberal, governing and opposition. It also needs to be borne in mind, however, that electors can react to the larger election contest as well as to the individual candidates representing the parties. A lively by-election contest between seasoned campaigners, for example, might well arouse the interest of both committed and uncommitted voters, thereby contributing to the transformation of a low-stimulus election into a high-stimulus one and increasing the level of turnout. Alternatively, misogynists bemoaning deteriorating social mores could well react to the presence of a female candidate, even if not from their own party, by abstaining out of principle. In short, an election contest as a whole can have its own distinctive identity and, in an effort to capture this identity, the effect of candidate characteristics in the aggregate, i.e., summed across all competing parties, is investigated. This analysis is then followed by a matching examination of the individual candidates by party.

The second observation is methodological and concerns the independent variables used in the regression analyses. These are constant throughout the chapter and, in addition to the long-term forces of country and partisanship, include candidates' age, sex, years in senior governmental office ('senior office'), exclusivity of electoral commitment to the constituency ('candidate exclusivity') and the prior holding of elective office in a branch of local government whose territorial jurisdiction encompassed all or part of the constituency ('local office'). In addition, candidates' years of parliamentary service to the constituency ('constituency MP') figures in the general election analysis and their years of parliamentary service to one or more other constituencies ('years as MP) in the by-election analysis. Two other variables originally scheduled for inclusion, the number of elections fought and the number of elections fought in the same constituency had to be dropped because of their excessive collinearity with each other and with one or more of the other independent variables. The choice among the collinear variables makes no difference to the findings, but what does differentiate them is their relative conceptual clarity and this was the criterion used to choose among them. Not least because it has been used in previous studies, the constituency MP variable, for example, is more easily and unambiguously interpreted than its collinear counterpart measuring the number of elections fought in the constituency.

Bearing these background notes in mind, the relationship between collective candidate characteristics and turnout levels can now be examined. It is summarised in Table 4.4; by way of reminder, the figures to the right of the variable names are standardised regression coefficients and to the left of them in parentheses the matching zero-order correlation coefficients. Immediately noticeable is the presence among the predictors of the electoral marginality variable despite its hardly being classifiable as a candidate characteristic. Its inclusion is intended to take account of the possibility that candidates with characteristics like senior political office to their credit are renominated in the party's safer seats since these are more readily won.[17] If such were the case, to exclude marginality would only mean that any relationships to emerge would risk being spurious since the effect of the attribute(s) in question might well, in reality, be a function of the closeness of the contest for the seat in the last parliamentary election.

Table 4.4: Standardised coefficients for the regression of turnout on collective candidate
characteristics by type of election

General election turnout			By-election turnout		
(.32)	Marginality	0.31	(.30)	Marginality	0.33
(-.22)	Sex	-0.18	(.23)	Country	0.23
(.07)	Country	0.15	(.20)	Partisanship	0.19
(-.21)	Local office	-0.15	(.22)	Sex	0.17
(-.15)	Constituency MP	-0.09		Candidate	
	$R^2 = 19.4$		(.11)	exclusivity	0.13
			(-.12)	Local office	-0.11
				$R^2 = 25.4$	

The not too surprising preeminence of marginality apart, the
outstanding feature of Table 4.4 is the apparent explanatory
importance of short-term candidate characteristics in both types of
election; they constitute at least half the significant predictors in
each equation. Moreover, when compared to the long-term forces of
country and partisanship, their effect is particularly marked in
general elections and it is tempting to argue that this is because the
candidates are somehow 'better' in this type of election. The
rationale for such an argument might be that since general elections
attract more experienced and visible candidates in the first place, it
is only to be expected that these candidates are better at mobilising
the electorate in the short term than are the less experienced
candidates to be found in by-elections. The relative 'weakness' of by-
election candidates could then be taken to explain why long-term
forces are more powerful in this type of election. Caution is advised,
however, since closer inspection of the table indicates that the
conclusions following from this argument would be misleading.

The major problem lies with the collective sex variable. Its
prominence in both equations might at first glance be taken to
vindicate the view that, in the absence of other orientating
mechanisms, electors respond to what they see in candidates in
making up their minds whether to vote or not. But the problem
with this line of reasoning is that it does not explain why the sex of
the candidates as a whole should have a negative effect on turnout
in general elections and a positive one in by-elections. There is, after
all, no *a priori* reason to believe that the electorate is schizophrenic
in this regard. Instead, the more likely solution to this puzzle lies in

the male domination of candidatures.

The result of coding females '0' and males '1' and then summing across the competing parties, is that the collective sex variable can become more or less synonomous with its candidate number counterpart. Indeed, as is plainly evident from these two variables being correlated at a value of 0.84 for general elections and 0.69 for by-elections, there is a substantial overlap between them. This overlap is especially pronounced in general elections where, the highly correlated candidate number variable not being included in the equation and male candidates being more numerous than in by-elections, sex comes to act as a surrogate for it. By contrast, Chapter 3 shows the candidate number variable to have no explanatory power in by-elections so that the appearance of the sex variable in Table 4.4 and with a directionally opposite effect to that of its general election counterpart can be taken as indicating a genuine by-election effect for sex. In other words, the sex variable *per se* has no meaning in the general election regression outcome in Table 4.4. Rather, it substitutes for the candidate number variable, which itself, it has been argued in Chapter 3, taps the long-term force of public disillusionment with the Conservative and Labour parties in an era of electoral abandonment of them.

This explanation of the directional inconsistency of the sex variable entails two larger conclusions. Firstly, insofar as non-candidate variables can now be seen to occupy the first three positions in each of the equations in Table 4.4, candidates as a whole can now be seen to play a less decisive explanatory role in both types of election than was first thought. They would still seem important enough in the aggregate, though, for any argument as to their essential superfluity to be discounted. Secondly, electors respond to the sex variable only in by-elections and, in all likelihood, this response is grounded in a combination of widespread sexual prejudice, low levels of interest and awareness and weak party cues, the latter two being typical of low-stimulus elections. More practically, this negative response to female candidates indicates that local party selectors have, at least in instrumental terms, some justification for any reticence that they might have in nominating female candidates as long as current sexual values and stereotypes prevail in British society.[18]

Also very noticeable in Table 4.4 is the consistently negative influence of two candidate attributes, constituency service and the holding of local government office, that were in fact expected to have the opposite effect on turnout levels. This reversal could have something to do with familiarity breeding contempt rather than respect and loyalty; simply being in office at whatever level of government makes a candidate party in the public eye to divisive decisions and non-decisions that gradually erode the coalition of popular support that brought him to office in the first place. In addition, it could be that a sense of frustration and futility grounded in a candidate's long tenure of a seat or his prior experience in local politics keeps opposition party supporters away from the polls. But while appealingly self-evident, the problem with these interpretations is that they make a number of demanding and generally untenable assumptions about the cognitive basis of the electorate as a whole's general response patterns to its political environment, especially its local one. While not wishing to argue that these assumptions are equally untenable for all electors, a more plausible and powerful general explanation is that the very fact of candidates having held elective office breeds apathy and lethargy in local party organisations regardless of how marginal the seat. That is, these two variables tap less candidate familiarity's effect on the electorate and more its deleterious effect on party electioneering machines. For the local office variable, the deterioration in its efficiency could well stem from internecine animosities rooted in the candidate's action, or inaction, when previously serving in local government. The constituency service variable's negative effect may also comprise an element of such animosity, but it is likely to be more the consequence of an electoral hegemony in the constituency which, the longer it lasts, leads all parties to become ever less successful at getting out their vote. Given that the constituency MP and local office variables were intended to measure candidates' personal followings and grass-roots support respectively, this interpretation of their actual effect does not mean that these phenomena do not exist. Rather, it indicates that, being less powerful, any positive effect that they have on turnout levels is overwhelmed, or 'swallowed up', by the depressant effect of what might be called organisational entropy.

That safety does breed lethargy is certainly the impression gained from Table 4.5. Starting from much the same general election baseline as safe seats, by-election turnout can be seen to be much higher in seats that change party hands in that by-election. What is more, its level in the succeeding general election even increases relative to the preceding one, which, the external evidence suggests, reflects less the response of a 'rational' electorate and more the extraordinary efforts of both defeated and victorious parties to

Table 4.5: Percentage turnout in seats changing and not changings hands in by-elections

	Turnout		
Seat changed *hands?*	*Preceding* *general election*	*By-* *election*	*Succeeding* *general election*
Yes	76.4	67.9	77.7
No	76.5	61.3	75.7

swing the unpredictable constituency their way after the 'upset' of the by-election contest. In short, the negative effects of the constituency service and local office variables are probably more safely interpreted as artefacts of organisational entropy in constituencies where entrenched candidates are well known to local party organisations than as the consequence of the repellent effect of voter familiarity with the candidates and their record in elective office. This interpretation is given further support* when Conservative- and Labour-held seats are compared later in this chapter.

The final observation to be made on Table 4.4 is negative in that it concerns the total absence from either equation of a national candidate effect, as measured by either or both of the senior political office and parliamentary service to another constituency variables. It might be argued that sex, acting as a surrogate measure of the nationwide erosion of confidence in the Conservative and Labour parties represents such an effect, but it is hardly candidate-specific. The point of this observation is that it emphasises the extent to which short-term local forces structure both general and by-election turnout. The character of this localism differs from one type of election to the other, however. In general elections, its impact is negative and, relating to prior tenure of local or national elective office, has been interpreted to reflect the influence of organisational entropy more than of the candidates themselves. Represented in by-elections only by the local office variable, entropy enjoys a less dominant explanatory role in them. What does happen in them, though, is that sex and candidate exclusivity, two characteristics that, inhering more immediately in the candidates as individuals, come to the fore and these are more clearly short-term in the sense of being specific to the by-election. Thus, it would seem the very openness of this type of election, the weakness of party cues in it and electors' low level of information and interest all combine to make the group of candidates on offer a more salient and influential reference point for the electorate at large than it is in general elections.

Table 4.6: Standardised coefficients for the regression of turnout on candidate characteristics by party and type of election

		General election turnout			
	Conservative			*Governing*	
(.32)	Marginality	0.34	(.32)	Marginality	0.31
(.07)	Country	0.14	(-.20)	Constituency MP	-0.19
	$R^2=12.5$		(.07)	Country	0.17
			(-.16)	Local office	-0.13
				$R^2=16.4$	
	Labour			*Opposition*	
(.32)	Marginality	0.33	(.32)	Marginality	0.35
(-.23)	Constituency MP	-0.24	(.07)	Country	0.17
(.07)	Country	0.17		$R^2=12.5$	
(-.02)	Senior office	0.13			
	$R^2=16.9$				
		By-election turnout			
	Conservative			*Governing*	
(.30)	Marginality	0.33	(.30)	Marginality	0.32
(.23)	Country	0.27	(.23)	Country	0.28
(.20)	Partisanship	0.19	(.20)	Partisanship	0.17
	$R^2=20.0$			$R^2=20.0$	
	Labour			*Opposition*	
(.30)	Marginality	0.31	(.30)	Marginality	0.33
(.23)	Country	0.29	(.23)	Country	0.27
(.20)	Partisanship	0.15	(.20)	Partisanship	0.16
(-.15)	Local office	-0.14	(-.14)	Local office	-0.13
(.17)	Candidate exclusivity	0.14		$R^2=21.9$	
	$R^2=23.5$				

Ranking fourth and fifth in both lists of significant predictors, the motive power of these aggregated candidate characteristics should not be overstated, however. Indeed, assuming that candidates are more visible collectively than they are individually, their lowly position raises the very real possibility that, being less salient, they will not have the same effect on turnout levels in the individual candidate regression equations. And, true to expectations, the limited impact of individual candidates in Britain's party-dominated electoral politics is confirmed in Table 4.6. This conclusion applies more or less equally to both general and by-elections, but there are some revealing, if minor, differences between both the individual parties and the two types of election.

Immediately noticeable is that the table has no general or by-election entry for Liberal candidates. This is because they proved to have no effect on the level of turnout in either type of election. Beyond this, the last chapter's conclusion as to the apparent explanatory importance of inter-party organisational disparities is strengthened by a comparison of the Conservative and Labour equations. The important point is that the personal attributes of Conservative candidates play no role at all in structuring constituency turnout levels in either type of election, whereas the reverse is true for Labour candidates. To take general elections first, MPs' length of incumbency, as measured by the constituency service variable, does not figure in the Conservative equation, while it is the second most important predictor in the Labour one. Thus, when the political stakes are high, as is the case in general elections, the Conservative party's superior organisation would seem to help it to overcome candidate hegemony's negative effect on the mobilisation of support. As for the Labour party, turnout in even its more marginal constituencies is very adversely affected by organisational entropy and probably compounding the party's congenitally poor organisation in this regard are the strained relations that commonly exist between Labour MPs and their often more radical constituency parties. Backed by a party philosophy advocating deference to established authority, the Conservative MP rarely encounters such problems and so is more often in control of his constituency party. The result is that the local party machine is more easily and efficiently mobilised on both his and the national party's behalf in election campaigns.

It stands to reason that the more efficient the organisational mobilisation of support, the less scope there is for competing forces to make their effect felt on turnout. Thus, the relative inefficiency of their organisation means that Labour candidates can to some extent compensate for this disadvantage with their personal qualities, more extensive advertising, or whatever. This is probably the essential reason why Labour candidates' being Privy Councillors boosts turnout. To the limited extent that it can be said to have an independent net effect in British electoral politics, therefore, an MP's personal following might be best thought of as a 'fallback' phenomenon in the sense that it affects turnout only when the larger party is weak, in this case organisationally.

A second, and directly related, interesting feature of general elections is that candidate hegemony has a similarly negative effect for governing party candidates, who can be either Conservative or Labour; the longer the governing party's candidate has held the seat, the lower the general election turnout. In contrast to the situation with Labour candidates, however, government hegemony's depressant effect probably relates to the wave of anti-government sentiment that commonly sweeps the country at election time as well as to organisational entropy. After all, more of the general election contests in this population have taken place under Conservative governments (140 as opposed to 100 under Labour governments) and in Conservative seats (126 as opposed to 113 in Labour seats and one in a Liberal seat) so that the negative effect of governing candidates' incumbency cannot be put down to their coming from the party with the congenitally poorer organisation. As with the Labour party, nonetheless, the senior office variable would have crept into the governing party equation in Table 4.6 with a beta weight of 0.11 had the inclusion criterion been a little less stringent. In weakening party commitment, in other words, anti-government feeling opens the way for candidates' personal qualities to have an effect on turnout. Once again, then, the precondition of a personal following stimulating turnout is that, whether for reason of poor organisation, weakened popular commitment, or whatever, the influence of long-standing party cues and loyalties on the public's electoral behaviour be weakened.

The broad conclusion to be drawn from this interpretation of general election turnout, then, is that the characteristics of individual candidates have no generalised role to play in its explanation. Any effect that they do have is intermittent, always secondary to the competitiveness of the seat and crucially conditioned in particular by the identity of the party for which the candidate is standing. This conclusion applies even more forcefully in by-elections where marginality, country and partisanship are unfailingly the principal predictors of turnout. The only other variable to appear more than once and to be consistently signed is local office and, as argued earlier, its negative effect is not likely to be the consequence of popular disapproval of local politicians 'rationally' discouraging electors from taking up their option to vote in by-elections. Instead, it is more likely to be a function of something like rivalries within the local party producing less than a wholehearted endorsement of the candidate at election time.[19]The absence of even the most sporadic by-election effect for either the senior office or prior parliamentary service variables contrasts with the situation in general elections and underlines the last chapter's conclusion as to the relatively national character of the general election turnout dynamic. Just as with political context in the previous chapter, by-elections emerge as events that tend to take place in a short-term political vacuum insofar as their turnout dynamic is largely immune to the short-term attributes of the individual candidates.

Before using the analysis up to this point to generate some final conclusions about candidates' effect on parliamentary election turnout levels, it is worth considering the proposition that the kind of global analysis presented in Table 4.6 is potentially misleading since its thrust is misdirected. The basis of this proposition is that a candidate's influence will in some degree be a function of his saliency to the constituency electorate and this saliency will itself be a function of his visibility to, and reputation with, that electorate. Now since the incumbent party's candidate is likely to be more visible precisely because of the asset of incumbency, it could be that he will be in a far stronger position to influence turnout levels. To test this possibility of a selective candidate effect, the exercise of the last chapter is now repeated and the population of constituencies divided into subgroups of, firstly, Conservative- and Labour-held seats and, secondly, government- and opposition-held ones.

Table 4.7 compares the Conservative and Labour seats groupings and two features of it are immediately striking. The first is the absence again of any entries for the Liberal party; its candidates just have no effect on the level of general or by-election turnout in either type of seat. The second is how similar the regression outcomes are to those for the population of by-election constituencies as a whole (compare Table 4.6). Broadly speaking, organisational weakness, as tapped by the constituency MP for general elections and the local office variable for by-elections, are once again the dominant candidate characteristics in Labour seats, but figure not at all in Conservative ones. The same sharp disparity characterises Conservative and Labour candidates in Table 4.6 and leads

Table 4.7: Standardised coefficients for the regression of turnout on candidate characteristics by Conservative and Labour incumbency and type of election

		General election turnout			
Conservative incumbency			*Labour incumbency*		
Conservative			*Conservative*		
(.49)	Marginality	0.52	(.20)	Marginality	0.25
(.09)	Partisanship	0.16		Candidate	
	$R^2 = 26.9$		(-.23)	exclusivity	-0.23
			(.19)	Country	0.22
			(-.22)	Local office	-0.16
				$R^2 = 17.7$	
Labour			*Labour*		
(.49)	Marginality	0.51	(.19)	Country	0.29
(.09)	Partisanship	0.17	(-.22)	Constituency MP	-0.28
	Candidate		(-.14)	Local office	-0.20
(-.03)	exclusivity	-0.14	(.20)	Marginality	0.20
	$R^2 = 28.5$		(.04)	Senior office	0.15
				$R^2 = 19.1$	

		By-election turnout			
Conservative incumbency			*Labour incumbency*		
Conservative			*Conservative*		
(.30)	Partisanship	0.33	(.32)	Marginality	0.39
(.26)	Marginality	0.27	(.26)	Country	0.31
	$R^2 = 16.7$		(-.25)	Local office	-0.22
				$R^2 = 26.2$	
Labour			*Labour*		
(.26)	Partisanship	0.27	(.26)	Country	0.36
(.30)	Marginality	0.25	(.32)	Marginality	0.36
	Candidate		(-.23)	Local office	-0.22
(.28)	exclusivity	0.22		$R^2 = 25.9$	
	$R^2 = 21.0$				

inevitably to the conclusion that to the extent candidates do have an influence on turnout, it is only those of the incumbent party's candidate that do so.

This conclusion might at first sight seem to be undermined by the fact that a 'new' variable, candidate exclusivity, emerges to depress general election turnout in both Conservative- and Labour-held seats. Not figuring in either the Conservative or Labour equations in Table 4.6, this variable might be taken to signal the existence of a surge of general election support for candidates faithfully pursuing their parliamentary ambition through the same constituency. Such a conclusion would be erroneous, however, because the minimum condition for its validity is that the relationship be positively signed. As it is, its sign is negative. What is more, since it is a relationship that is to be found only for each major party candidate in the other major party's seats, its negative character is more likely a reflection of the impregnability of the constituency for the non-incumbent major party. It is precisely in such safe seats that turnout is lowest and two types of opposition party candidate are to be found fighting them. The first is the ambitious, career-minded aspirant who is 'learning his trade' by making his political debut in an unwinnable seat. The second type is most commonly found in the Liberal party but is not unknown among major party candidates and he is the local party loyalist who is drafted in, often more than once, to 'carry the party flag' in a hopeless contest. Rarely having stood elsewhere in the past, both types of candidates would show a high, if not total, level of electoral commitment to the constituency, even though, in the latter case, this commitment testifies more to the candidate's party loyalty than to his political ambition. Whatever their reason(s) for standing, though, their negative impact on turnout is probably more accurately interpreted as being the consequence of the other party's being safely esconced in the constituency rather than of the electorate's negative appraisal of them as parliamentary candidates.

But if the personal attributes of the candidates do play some role in the explanation of general election turnout, they have a less important one in by-elections. Validating the interpretation of local office as a measure of organisational entropy is the fact that this variable figures only in the equations for Labour seats, the party that is the more prone to factionalism and the less well equipped to cope with it. The only other short-term characteristic to appear in the by-election equations is candidate exclusivity, but it appears only once so caution advises that not too much be read into it.

In sum, then, candidates' attributes can, and do, independently influence turnout levels, but it is an influence that is not strong in Britain's party-dominated electoral process. The few instances where these characteristics have been important suggest, moreover, that their influence makes itself felt not when candidates are strong in the sense of being, say, nationally prominent, but when the influence of party is weak. That candidate characteristics appear more frequently in the Labour equations, both general and by-election, suggests that organisational shortcomings contribute to this weakness, but Table 4.7 indicates that a second factor mediating the emergence of a candidate influence is the ideological gap between the parties, as measured by the level of partisanship in the electorate. This variable appears in every Conservative equation and in none of the Labour ones. It is even more powerful than marginality in the determination of by-election turnout in Conservative seats. It would seem once again, therefore, that Conservative constituency electorates are more sensitive and responsive to their immediate party political environment. Labour constituency electorates, on the other hand, give no indication of being equally sensitive to this environment and their relative passivity then contributes to their turnout levels becoming relatively open to influence in the short term from candidate attributes tapping organisational entropy.[20]

This party-based explanation of candidate characteristics' limited influence is confirmed when the focus of attention is switched from a comparison of Conservative- and Labour-held seats to one of government- and opposition-held ones. Differences of emphasis between general and by-elections also emerge more clearly. To take general elections first, Table 4.8 confirms the last chapter's conclusion as to the fundamental dissimilarity of the turnout dynamic in government and opposition seats. Insofar as marginality is the only variable to influence turnout in opposition seats, it seems that the electorate is moved by the immediate circumstances of a general election only when it is able to pass its judgment on the government directly. The lack of an effect for the partisanship or candidate characteristic variables in opposition seats suggests once again that the opposition party is not a salient reference point for British electors and that the traditional adversarial model of the British electoral process adds little to our understanding of the general election turnout dynamic.[21] This conclusion is only reinforced by the explanatory irrelevance of opposition candidates in government seats.

The characteristics of opposition party candidates may not be very important at all, but those of governing party candidates are, at least in seats held by the government. The constituency MP variable has been argued to reflect the organisational entropy that will almost inevitably envelop a repeatedly successful constituency

Table 4.8: Standardised coefficients for the regression of turnout on candidate characteristics by government and opposition incumbency and type of election

---

General election turnout

Government incumbency			*Opposition incumbency*		
Governing			*Governing*		
(-.23)	Constituency MP	-0.32	(.23)	Marginality	0.27
(.37)	Marginality	0.30		$R^2=5.2$	
(-.23)	Local office	-0.22			
(.08)	Senior office	0.20			
(.06)	Country	0.17			
(.05)	Candidate exclusivity	0.16			
	$R^2=26.8$				
Opposition			*Opposition*		
(.37)	Marginality	0.39	(.23)	Marginality	0.26
(-.14)	Candidate exclusivity	-0.17		$R^2=5.2$	
	$R^2=16.1$				

By-election turnout

Government incumbency			*Opposition incumbency*		
Governing			*Governing*		
(.26)	Marginality	0.29	(.38)	Marginality	0.39
(.24)	Country	0.28	(.19)	Country	0.21
(.18)	Partisanship	0.18	(-.25)	Local office	-0.20
	$R^2=17.8$			$R^2=25.7$	
Opposition			*Opposition*		
(.24)	Country	0.28	(.38)	Marginality	0.39
(.26)	Marginality	0.27	(.19)	Country	0.24
(.18)	Partisanship	0.17	(.21)	Partisanship	0.20
	$R^2=17.8$		(-.21)	Local office	-0.18
				$R^2=28.8$	

party and that this variable takes precedence over marginality in government seats points to the existence of an abstentionist reaction against the incumbent government that even the organisational effort induced by the risk of losing the seat is not able to overcome.

Security may well breed complacency, but there is no reason why insecurity should do the same unless constituency parties are caught up by forces that are largely beyond their control. What would seem to be happening, therefore, is that, even in marginal seats, organisational complacency is compounded by popular dissatisfaction with the government and this combination weakens, albeit temporarily, the ties between party and supporter and thereby encourages abstentionism. To state this conclusion more prosaically, governing party supporters would seem to show their dissatisfaction by 'voting with their feet' and more of them do so the safer is the seat for the government in the sense of the longer the incumbent candidate has held it.

This is not to argue that the more entrenched the governing party is in a constituency, the more likely are its supporters alone to abstain. Any party's long-standing hegemony in a constituency will also breed frustration and abstentionism among opposition party supporters. What does seem to happen, though, is that, enjoying the advantage of incumbency, the governing party candidate is able to influence the general election turnout behaviour of the constituency electorate insofar as his personal base of support serves to offset to some extent the anti-government sentiment making for abstentionism. Thus, especially when nationally prominent and monogamous in his parliamentary service to the one constituency, the government's candidate has a substantial, independent ability to stimulate turnout. His ability in this regard should not be exaggerated, however; it is secondary to, and conditioned by, his party's weakened hold on its constituency electorates.

The second, and related, noteworthy feature of Table 4.8 is that it again shows the relationship, weak as it may be, between candidate characteristics and turnout levels to be substantially different for the two types of election. The simple fact of the matter is that, be they from the governing or opposition party, candidates are largely irrelevant to the explanation of by-election turnout. Marginality and country are always the preeminent explanatory variables and partisanship ranks third in both government incumbency equations and one opposition one, indicating that government supporters especially are less likely to abstain the wider the partisan gap between the parties. The one exception to the observation of candidate irrelevance is the presence, as the last-ranked variable, of local office in both opposition incumbency equations. Its effect would seem to indicate that a degree of organisational apathy grips even the more marginal opposition seats in by-elections, probably at least partly because so little is at stake in them. The parties in government seats, on the other hand, will take pains to guard against such apathy because they will be more sensitive to the effect on their credibility of a poor by-election peformance by the government; the government's will suffer and the opposition's be enhanced.

It can only be concluded, therefore, that to the limited extent that each responds to candidate characteristics at all, the turnout dynamic in the two types of election responds to different forces. In particular, general election turnout proves especially sensitive to a variable that is not even applicable in by-elections, namely, the incumbent MP's length of parliamentary service to the constituency. But otherwise being predicated on a series of weak relationships, the difference should be seen more generally as one of degree rather than kind and not be overstated. After all, albeit that its effect is weaker, the local office variable is the by-election counterpart to the constituency MP one. Still, especially when seen against the background of a weak candidate effect overall, it is a difference that is sufficiently pronounced to confirm the last chapter's conclusion that the by-election turnout dynamic cannot be dismissed as a mere carbon copy of that found in general elections. At least as far as the candidates are concerned, the crucial difference is that incumbents can accumulate a personal following that helps to offset general election abstentionism rooted in anti-government sentiment or the inadequate organisational mobilisation of support. Not having been incumbent in the constituency, though, by-election candidates have no similar following there even though they too might be national political figures. An MP's personal following, in other words, is not transferable from constituency to consituency even though it might be based on his national political prominence.

Rate of Change of Turnout

Going by the criteria established in the last chapter, this section of the analysis should comprise the following set of independent variables: country, marginality, change in marginality, partisanship, change in partisanship, the range of by-election candidate characteristic variables and the change measures on this same group of attributes. As it transpires, however, the cross-sectional and change measures on the candidate exclusivity, local office and sex variables are inter-correlated to a degree that precludes the inclusion of both measures in the regression analysis.[22] Faced with the need to choose, the cross-sectional measures were retained for two reasons. First, since a good number of by-election candidates also contested the preceding general election in the same constituency, the notion of candidate change is not always very meaningful.[23] Second, and relatedly, the last chapter indicated that the rate of change of by-election turnout was in fact little influenced by corresponding change in the contextual predictor variables. So as not to risk underestimating any effect that candidates' personal attributes may have, therefore, the best strategy is to keep their cross-sectional versions in the analysis to come.

Table 4.9: Standardised coefficients for the regression of turnout change on collective candidate characteristics[*]

	Inter-election turnout change	
(-.36)	Δ Marginality	-0.49
(-.17)	Marginality	-0.44
(-.25)	Country	-0.21
(-.21)	Δ Constituency MP	-0.19
(.16)	Δ Partisanship	0.18
(-.34)	Sex	-0.15
	R^2=40.9	

[*]Δ denotes change

Table 4.9 summarises the impact of the collective candidate characteristic variables on the rate of change of turnout between parliamentary elections. As in the last chapter, the outcome is similar to that for its cross-sectional by-election counterpart (see Table 4.4). Yet close inspection of the table indicates that turnout change has its own distinctive dynamic. Marginality can be seen to be again by far and away the most powerful explanatory variable with the seat's becoming more competitive in the by-election being an especially effective antidote to turnout decline. Women candidates in by-elections can again be seen to have a negative effect on turnout; their presence makes its decline between elections just that little bit bigger. Nor can this finding be dismissed as an artefact of the collective sex variable acting as a surrogate for public disillusion, as measured by the number of candidates. If such were the case, sex's relationship to turnout change would be positive since turnout could be expected to drop further as public disillusion escalated. That the relationship is in fact negative would seem to indicate a genuine candidate effect for the collective sex variable.

Also influential is the constituency service variable. Earlier in this chapter, this variable was argued to be functioning as a measure of organisational entropy resulting from a constituency's being safe for the incumbent candidate. That the length of incumbency in fact discourages turnout decline in Table 4.9 does not now contradict this interpretation of its meaning. Rather, it indicates that once the incumbent does depart, the organisational mobilisation of the vote in the constituency slips into a higher gear as both incumbent and non-incumbent parties seek to influence turnout patterns to their advantage in a contest that is more open than for some time precisely because there is no candidate with the advantage of incumbency. Given, however, that entropy was not a problem in Conservative seats in the first place, the rate of change of turnout in them might well not be affected by how long their former MP had held the seat.

Disaggregating the population of seats into Conservative- and Labour-held groupings shows the constituency service variable in fact to figure in both groups of seats and, judging by the correlation coefficients, to be about equally important in both of them.[24] If anything, it is Labour that seems slightly better at recovering from the entropic effect of incumbency to stem the tide of turnout decline in its own seats. This is probably because it generally starts from a lower baseline of internal unity and organisational efficiency in the first place. The fact that the party organisation is able to unite behind a new candidate and to concentrate its mobilisation effort in one or or two constituencies rather than spread it over more than six hundred of them means that the party's impact on the rate of change of turnout will be little different from the Conservative party's. If this is the case, the small advantage enjoyed by the Labour party could well be due to the fact that its departing MPs tend to have held the seat a little longer than their Conservative counterparts, an average 13.3 years and 12.5 years respectively.

The overall effect of this burst of enthusiasm and flurry of activity should not be overstated, however. There is certainly no evidence that it is sufficient to disguise, even if temporarily, the habitually poorer mobilisation effort in Labour seats. Indeed, the two parties' differential success in getting voters to the polls, as reflected in the performance of the marginality variable, can be seen

Table 4.10: Standardised coefficients for the regression of turnout change on candidate characteristics by Conservative and Labour incumbency and type of election[*]

	Inter-election turnout change				
Conservative incumbency			*Labour incumbency*		
Conservative			*Conservative*		
(-.41)	Δ Marginality	-0.62	(-.21)	Marginality	-0.55
(.10)	Δ Partisanship	0.33	(-.34)	Δ Marginality	-0.54
(-.09)	Marginality	-0.29	(-.22)	Country	-0.27
(-.24)	Country	-0.18		R^2=37.2	
(-.18)	Δ Constituency MP	-0.15			
	R^2=38.3				
Labour			*Labour*		
(-.41)	Δ Marginality	-0.62	(-.21)	Marginality	-0.58
(.10)	Δ Partisanship	0.33	(-.34)	Δ Marginality	-0.50
(-.09)	Marginality	-0.26	(-.22)	Country	-0.28
(-.24)	Country	-0.20	(-.22)	Δ Constituency MP	-0.26
(-.27)	Candidate exclusivity	-0.17		R^2=42.5	
	R^2=39.5				

[*] Δ denotes change

once again to be the principal feature distinguishing the pattern of turnout change in the two groups of constituencies. To put it simply, we would expect the prospect of a seat's becoming more marginal and, hence, losable to be an equally effective deterrent to turnout decline no matter which party held the constituency. Table 4.10 shows, though, that the increased competitiveness of the seat is the most effective antidote to turnout decline only in Conservative seats. In Labour seats, it is the marginality of the seat in the preceding general election that plays this role. It is as if this party is not as able to get out its supporters to ward off the upcoming threat to their continued tenure of the seat. Nor can this complacency be explained by the lack of a need to do so. With an average 23.2 per cent of the by-election vote separating it from the second-placed party as opposed to the smaller 21.6 per cent in Conservative seats, Labour strongholds may remain relatively safe. Nonetheless, the difference in their margin of safety is hardly sufficient to encourage it to choose to be more complacent than the Conservative party in getting out its vote, especially when by-elections themselves are so unpredictable in their outcomes. It is likely, therefore, that the threat of losing the seat does not have the same effect on turnout change in Labour seats not because of a conscious choice on the part of the incumbent party, but in part because its organisational efforts to maintain its general election support are congenitally less successful.

Apart from the constituency service variable, there is little evidence of an important role for candidates in the explanation of turnout change in either group of seats. But what is worth noting is that partisanship appears once again in Conservative seats, but not in Labour ones. Interestingly, though, it is the change version of this variable that figures in the equations, which means that the less partisan the party political environment becomes, the bigger is the drop in turnout in Conservative seats. The earlier conclusion of a more responsive electorate in Conservative seats is suggested once again.

Table 4.11: Standardised coefficients for the regression of turnout change on candidate characteristics by government and opposition incumbency and type of election[*]

	Inter-election turnout change				
	Government incumbency			*Opposition incumbency*	
	Governing			*Governing*	
(-.06)	Marginality	-0.44	(-.30)	Δ Marginality	-0.59
(-.29)	Δ Marginality	-0.40	(-.36)	Marginality	-0.50
(-.30)	Country	-0.29	(.18)	Local office	0.19
(.31)	Δ Partisanship	0.27		R^2=35.3	
(-.25)	Δ Constituency MP	-0.24			
	R^2=34.6				
	Opposition			*Opposition*	
(-.29)	Δ Marginality	-0.47	(-.30)	Δ Marginality	-0.53
(-.06)	Marginality	-0.40	(-.36)	Marginality	-0.51
(-.30)	Country	-0.30	(.23)	Local office	0.17
(.31)	Δ Partisanship	0.17	(-.14)	Δ Constituency MP	-0.16
	R^2=30.7			R^2=38.8	

Since candidate characteristics do generally have such little effect on the rate of change of turnout, it might be expected that much the same picture would emerge for government and opposition seats as does for Conservative and Labour ones. This expectation is fully realised. Again, the marginality variables can be seen to dominate all four equations in Table 4.11, although it is also noteworthy that government seats are once again like Labour ones in that it is the cross-sectional version of this variable that is preeminent. Governments' general election supporters, it would seem, become disillusioned with their party and are less easily mobilised at by-election time with the result that their party's hold on the seat becomes less firm, a process possibly helped along by anti-government sentiment ensuring that opposition party supporters in the general election do not abstain at the same rate. Not too surprisingly, the only other variable to figure in both groups of seats is constituency service; the longer the departing MP has held the seat, the harder all parties try to get out their general election supporters in the relatively open by-election contest. Probably because so little is at stake in them, the effect of these mobilisation efforts are diluted in opposition seats by the incumbent or governing party's candidate having held local office; organisational entropy would seem to be less easily overcome when the government is not 'on trial' in a by-election.

Conclusion

Insofar as their various attributes figure frequently and often prominently in this chapter's different tables, it would seem appropriate to conclude that candidates, contrary to conventional wisdom, play a significant role in structuring constituency turnout patterns in British parliamentary elections. If overstated, however, this conclusion would run a great risk of being misleading. The problem this chapter encounters is that the relationships between turnout and certain candidate characteristics are not always in the expected direction. Moreover, the form that they do take lends itself to a more plausible interpretation if it is conceded that the candidate characteristic in question is, in empirical terms, measuring some party feature other than an election-specific attribute of the candidate it puts up in a particular constituency for a particular election. To complicate matters, this problem consistently besets the two most frequently influential candidate variables, parliamentary service to the constituency and prior holding of elective office in some constituency-related branch of local government.

Each being intended to measure some form of personal following founded in familiarity with, and service to, the constituency, it was anticipated that both these variables would have a positive influence on all three dimensions of turnout. When they do cross the threshold of significance, however, their relationship to turnout is, in fact, unfailingly negative. The conclusion that immediately suggests itself is the more familiar a constituency is with a candidate, the more support ebbs away from him rather than flows to him. While not inconceivable, especially for political incompetents, the problem with this conclusion is that it flies in the face of accumulating evidence that elective office holders do on the whole accumulate a personal following that grows more or less with the length of time that they represent the constituency. It cannot even be argued that those longest incumbent see this support base erode as a result of 'outstaying their welcome'; the evidence just does not support this argument.[25] A more plausible interpretation, therefore, would seem to be that while incumbency may indeed generate a personal following, its more powerful effect is to encourage incumbent and non-incumbent parties in even the more marginal constituencies to become less assiduous in their organisational mobilisation of the vote as elections increasingly take on the aura of being foregone conclusions. This 'organisational' interpretation is vindicated by the fact that the longer the departing MP has been incumbent, the lower the drop in turnout between general and by-elections - presumably not because the incumbent party's by-election candidate, who will be new to the constituency, is a greater drawing card than his immediate predecessor, but because the competing parties fire up their engines for a contest that has at last become relatively open.

Importantly, though, to opt for this entropic interpretation of the overall relationship is not to argue that candidates play no role in bringing it about. Almost certainly, one reason why party organisations run down is that policy disagreements, personality clashes and the like stimulate some degree of membership disaffection from the office holder and weaken the organisation as a whole's commitment to his reelection. Familiarity breeding disaffection is, of course, a process that is as likely to afflict local politicians as it is national ones. A problem with the aggregate data used herein is that they do not allow for the separation of this disaffection from what might be called 'natural' entropy. This chapter's analysis does, however, provide other evidence to suggest the confident conclusion of a direct candidate effect, even if it is not uniform across parties or turnout dimensions.

This analysis started with the hypothesis that candidates will be important when other party stimuli are weak. This was the basis of the expectation that they would make their presence felt less in the explanation of general election turnout and more in that of by-election turnout and turnout change. And, indeed, insofar as candidates' sex affected both these latter dimensions of turnout, at least when candidates are treated as a collectivity, some support was provided for this hypothesis. A somewhat different picture emerges, however, when candidates are treated individually. The constituency MP and local office variables apart, there is no evidence of anything like a consistent candidate effect across the three turnout dimensions. The strongest such effect of all is to be found, contrary to expectations, in general elections despite the fact that the candidate is only one of several powerful party stimuli acting on the turnout dynamic. Again, however, it is an effect that is sporadic rather than consistent and it takes the form essentially of an incumbent candidate's tenure of senior political governmental offsetting low turnout when his party is weak. Broadly speaking, organisational weakness allows this apparent personal following to emerge for Labour candidates and anti-government sentiment for governing party candidates. There is finally some weak indication that the more local a candidate (in the sense of being electorally committed to the constituency being fought), the more likely he will boost general election turnout in seats where his party is *not* incumbent. In other words, the larger the proportion of other constituencies contested by the candidate for the non-incumbent party, the lower the turnout. This relationship could be interpreted to mean that party organisations and/or supporters have a tendency to react against 'carpet-bagging' candidates when their party's tenure of the seat is not at risk.

It is also interesting to note that, broadly speaking, it is 'national' forces (public disillusion and tenure of senior political office) that fuel the general election turnout dynamic, whereas, not enjoying the personal following that derives from the advantage of incumbency, nothing about the individual candidates exercises a similar effect on by-election turnout and turnout change. Treated as a collectivity, though, candidates become a more salient reference point for electors and influence both these turnout dimensions and it is their 'local' characteristics (sex and candidate exclusivity) that do so. Moreover, to the extent that the sex variable is the only one to affect both these turnout dimensions, it is relevant that its effect is stronger for turnout change (a simple correlation of -0.34 as opposed to 0.22 for by-election turnout). Thus, there is some evidence confirming Chapter 3's conclusion that it is the rate of change dynamic that has the strongest local component of all three turnout dimensions. This evidence, though, is very weak and it is so because the short-term candidate characteristics examined in this chapter have no more than a limited impact on constituency turnout patterns.

The most general conclusion to be drawn from this chapter, then, is that short-term candidate attributes have no generalised role to play in the explanation of constituency turnout patterns. Indeed, it has shown that individual candidates consistently come to the explanatory fore in Britain not in certain types of election, but when parties are weak and in general elections only. This weakness allows incumbent candidates to swim against the tide and for their personal followings to emerge as a significant influence on turnout. Being new to the constituency, by-election candidates have not had the time to cultivate a personal support base there. Nor do they seem able directly to import one founded on their prior parliamentary service or attainment of senior political office. Given Britain's party-dominated polity, however, such weakness is unlikely ever to be serious enough to give the candidate anything more than a limited electoral importance in his own right. Nonetheless, his contribution to the mobilisation of support could mean the difference between a beleaguered party's winning or losing a closely fought seat. Being of limited importance, in other words, is not the same as being irrelevant.

Notes

[1]Ivor Jennings, *Party Politics* (Cambridge: Cambridge University Press, 1961), pp. 260-61.

[2]Austin Mitchell, 'The Local Campaign, 1977-79' in Robert M. Worcester and Martin Harrop, eds, *Political Communications* (London: Allen & Unwin, 1982), p. 36.   An academic statement of this viewpoint is Michael Steed, 'The Results Analysed' in David Butler and Dennis Kavanagh, *The British General Election of February 1974*, p. 335.

[3]Mitchell, 'The Local Campaign', p. 38. This statement is very reminiscent of the anonymous elector who candidly declared: 'I would vote for a pig if my party put one up.' Quoted in David Butler, *The British General Election of 1951* (London: Macmillan, 1952), p. 173.

[4]See John Bochel and David Denver, 'Candidate Selection in the Labour Party: What the Selectors Seek', *British Journal of Political Science*, 13 (1983), 45-70.

[5]Austin Ranney, *Pathways to Parliament: Candidate Selection in Britain* (London: Macmillan, 1965), p. 35.   See also Michael Rush, *The Selection of Parliamentary Candidates* (London: Nelson, 1969).

[6]Four treatments of this phenomenon are Bruce E. Cain, John A. Ferejohn and Morris P. Fiorina, 'The Constituency Service Basis of the Personal Vote for U.S. Representatives and British Members of Parliament', *American Political Science Review*, 78 (1984), 110-25; Patrick Dunleavy and Christopher T. Husbands, *British Democracy at the Crossroads* (London: Allen & Unwin, 1985), pp. 204-08; Anthony Mughan, 'Towards a Political Explanation of Government Vote Losses in Midterm By-Elections', *American Political Science Review*, 80 (1986); and Philip M. Williams, 'Two Notes on the British Electoral System', *Parliamentary Affairs*, 20 (1966-67), 13-30.

[7]See Clive S. Bean, 'The Impact of Short-Term Forces on the Vote' in Hyam Gold, ed., *New Zealand Politics in Perspective* (Auckland: Longman Paul, 1985), 334-47 and Harold D. Clarke, Jane Jenson, Lawrence LeDuc and Jon H. Pammett, *Political Choice in Canada* (Toronto: McGraw-Hill Ryerson, 1979), pp. 321-55 & 373-74.

[8]The classic statement of this party style is Otto Kircheimer, 'The Transformation of Western European Party Systems' in Joseph LaPalombara and Myron Weiners, eds, *Political Parties and Political Development* (Princeton, N.J.: Princeton University Press, 1966), 177-220.

[9]Cain et al., 'The Constituency Service Basis of the Personal Vote', p. 111.

[10]MPs may also, of course, arouse the antagonism of their constituents and they are more likely to do so, the longer they stay in office. The concluding section of this chapter addresses the question of whether there is any evidence that MPs do in fact 'outstay their welcome' in this way. See footnote 25 below in particular.

[11]In this population of constituencies with unchanging boundaries, there have only been three by-elections in which one of the candidates has represented the constituency in Parliament before. These are Buckinghamshire, Wycombe (4/11/52), Bristol, South-East (4/5/61) and Merton, Mitcham and Morden (3/6/82).

[12]The 240 by-elections comprising this study in fact include 26 Conservative by-election candidates with previous experience as an MP, 22 Labour candidates and eight Liberal candidates. These numbers do not necessarily represent different individuals since some of their number fought more than one by-election contest in their reelection efforts.

[13]A good treatment of the circumstances leading up to, and surrounding, the formation of the SDP is Ian Bradley, *Breaking the Mould?* (Oxford: Martin Robertson, 1981). For the electoral alliance with the Liberals, see Ivor Crewe, 'Is Britain's Two-Party System Really about to Crumble? The Social Democratic-Liberal Alliance and the Prospects for Realignment', *Electoral Studies* 1, 275-313. The small number of by-elections (13) held after the formation of the Alliance means that Liberal and SDP candidates are treated synonomously herein and bracketed under the 'Liberal' heading.

[14]There are several examples of individuals who resign from Parliament or lose their seat and subsequently seek reentry by means of a by-election victory. A good example is the Right Honourable Roy Jenkins. As a very senior member of the Labour party, he resigned his Birmingham seat to become President of the European Commission and subsequently sought to reenter the House of Commons by contesting the Warrington and then Glasgow, Hillhead by-elections as an SDP candidate in the 1979-83 Parliament. More generally, the 240 cases forming the basis of this study include the by-election candidacies of five senior Conservative politicians, four Labour ones and three Liberal ones. These are not necessarily different individuals since some of their number fought more than one by-election in their efforts to get back into Parliament. Jenkins is an example.

[15]The local office variable employed herein performs only slightly differently from a similar one measuring candidates' experience of elective local office anywhere in Britain. The reasons for this similarity are essentially twofold. Firstly, many candidates are not geographically mobile so any local government office that they have held will be related to the constituency they are contesting. Secondly, the variable itself is not very discriminating since it would attribute a local connection to a parish councillor within a constituency at one extreme and a county councillor whose jurisdiction covered a large number of constituencies at the other. In the middle, there is the city councillor whose jurisdiction encompasses the several, perhaps ten or more, constituencies to be found within the boundaries of Britain's largest cities.

[16]It is arguable that more sensitive measures of a candidate's local connections are whether he was born in the constituency, whether he works

there, whether he has always lived there, and so on. This might well be true, but there is an insuperable problem in discovering this sort of information for all candidates over the three decades or so covered by this analysis. It is readily available for successful parliamentary aspirants in publications like *Who's Who*, but there is no similarly detailed source for unsuccessful ones. Indeed, the only source for them, and it is minimal in terms of information content, is the various editions of *The Times Guide to the House of Commons* and, supplemented by newspaper acounts of individual by-elections contests, this is where the candidate information in this data set comes from.

[17]There is, in fact, some evidence indicating the wisdom of this precaution and it shows interesting variation by party incumbency. In Conservative seats, for example, the simple correlation between preceding general election marginality and the number of years the party's by-election candidates have already spent in Parliament is -0.13, whereas this figure Labour candidates in Labour seats is 0.04. When it comes to the candidates' prior holding of senior political office, these figures are -0.20 and 0.06 respectively. In other words, Conservative selection committees in safe seats show some preference, perhaps under the urging of the national party leadership, for by-election candidates with prior parliamentary experience, especially at the senior office level. Labour selection committees in safe seats, on the other hand, are more likely to prefer candidates with local government experience, this variable's correlation with marginality for Labour candidates in Labour seats being -0.15 and for Conservative candidates in Conservative seats .01.

[18]This is not to say that overt sexual prejudice does inform the decisions of selection committees. The evidence available suggest that selectors in the reputedly more sexist of the two major parties, Labour, show no such prejudice and even believe that more women should be adopted as candidates. See Bochel and Denver, 'Candidate Selection in the Labour Party', pp. 54-55.

[19]Since marginality is controlled in the regression analysis, local office's negative impact in by-elections cannot be attributed to the tendency of Labour selection committees in safe seats (where turnout is low anyway) to prefer candidates with local government experience. Besides, the local office variable also has something of a negative effect for Conservative candidates, just failing to enter the Conservative by-election equation in Table 4.6 with a beta weight of -0.10.

[20]While Conservative electorates appear more sophisiticated, this explanation of partisanship's different effect is nonetheless oversimplified. Conservative electorates do not seem to respond to higher partisanship by becoming more faithful to the party incumbent in their constituency. The simple correlation between partisanship and the Conservative by-election vote in these seats being a negative -0.28, they appear, if anything, to become less faithful. With a matching correlation of 0.41, it is Labour that

apparently benefits from high partisanship, even in Conservative seats. But Labour's relative 'advantage' is not the most important reason for partisanship's stimulation of by-election turnout. If it were, then partisanship should have a net impact on turnout in Labour seats since its correlation with the parties' vote in them are very similar to those found in Conservative seats, 0.43 for Labour and -0.10 for Conservative. The basic reason for partisanship's not figuring in the Labour group of seats, however, concerns the different role played by the Liberal party in the two groups of seats. Where Conservatives are incumbent, the correlation between partisanship and the Liberal vote is 0.25 and the matching figure in Labour seats is 0.03. This difference becomes more meaningful when seen against the background of the middle class being less willing than the working class to view politics in terms of class conflict. See David Butler and Donald Stokes, *Political Change in Britain*, 2nd ed. (London: Macmillan, 1974), 90-94. That is, disgruntled Conservative supporters appear more likely to respond to class polarisation by voting Liberal rather than abstaining and risking the loss of the seat to Labour. In Labour seats, by contrast, such supporters may simply abstain and thereby help to cancel out partisanship's overall turnout effect.

[21]This conclusion is supported by the fact that trends in the opposition party's popularity do not affect the size of the drop in the government's vote between general and by-elections. See Mughan, 'Towards a Political Explanation'.

[22]The simple correlations between the cross-sectional and change measures on the collective candidate characteristics of sex, local office and exclusivity are 0.62, 0.69 and 0.73 respectively. This problem is even worse for Conservative party candidates where these same figures are 0.82, 0.74 and 0.85 respectively. For an account of the dangers of using stepwise regression in the presence of such multicollinearity, see Eric A. Hanushek and John A. Jackson, *Statistical Methods for Social Scientists* (New York: Academic Press, 1977), pp. 95-96.

[23]Calculated over the 242 constituencies whose boundaries remained unchanged between the general elections preceding and succeeding the by-election and over the Conservative, Labour and Liberal parties, 113 by-election candidates contested the preceding general election and 190 the succeeding general election. These totals are not made up of different people since the same candidate sometimes fought two or more of the three elections and is consequently counted twice in the total figures.

[24]It will be noticed immediately that the individual candidate regressions for the population of constituencies as a whole are not reported in the text. The decision not to present them was taken for two reasons. First, to have done so would be an essentially redundant exercise since they add nothing to the argument suggested by Tables 4.9, 4.10 and 4.11. It has already been observed in the body of the chapter that this observation applies equally to the cross-sectional regressions for all constituencies

presented in Table 4.6. Second, and relatedly, the table is very complex and would only have served to interrupt the flow of the argument. A copy of the table can be obtained from me on request, however.

[25]This argument holds essentially that the relationship between length of incumbency and turnout is non-linear and I put it to the empirical test by including a quadratic term for the personal vote variables. This exercise did not improve the predictive power of any of the equations reported in this chapter. See also Dunleavy and Husbands, *British Democracy at the Crossroads*, pp. 206-08.

5   The National Standing of the Parties and Turnout

Introduction

In examining the effect of, first, the political context of parliamentary elections and, second, the candidates standing in them, the previous two chapters have concentrated for the most part on a number of important local factors that potentially impinge on turnout patterns. More specifically, their substantive focus has been the identification of which of these factors affect the mobilisation of party support on election day. It is important to remember, though, that Britain's political parties exist as national, as well as local, institutions. Moreover, of these two levels of identity, it is generally accepted that it is the national one that is the better defined in the electorate's eyes since '(p)olitics in Britain, to a remarkable degree, are based on the competition between cohesive parties which act together in the national legislature and offer unified appeals for the support of the mass electorate.'[1] This is the aspect of British political culture that underpins the conventional wisdom to the effect that the country's electoral politics are national in character and orientation. A typical statement of this viewpoint is: 'Voters pay much more attention to the national campaign and leaders than to the local campaign and candidates.'[2]

Rooted as it is in general elections, this characterisation of the dynamic of British electoral politics is not too overdrawn in that particular context, although this analysis' demonstration of the importance for general election turnout patterns of the constituency characteristics of marginality and party incumbency cautions against too ready and uncritical an acceptance of it. Caution is transformed into something more like scepticism, however, when, characterising them as 'mini' general elections, this same dynamic is held to apply more or less equally to by-elections. According to this argument, the defining characteristic of by-elections is that their outcome serves as a barometer of national public opinion on the performance of the government in office. Herman Finer, for example, describes them as 'invaluable periodical referenda on the action of the government'.[3] This interpretation of their significance is based on two related assumptions that seem reasonable in the British context. The first of them is that governments will decline in popularity simply by taking and implementing decisions that are not always acceptable to all elements of the support coalition that brought them to office in the first place. The second is that since the British electorate is relatively unmoved by local forces, the government's loss of support will manifest itself in by-election outcomes since these will accurately reflect trends in national public opinion. Nor is this an interpretation to be taken lightly. By-elections' imputed role as a referendum on the government's performance is the essential reason for their attracting, especially when involving government seats, media attention that is usually out of all proportion to their immediate political significance. Rarely, for example, does a government's parliamentary majority hang in the balance in a by-election. The popularity of this interpretation also helps to explain why their outcomes are taken very seriously by governments in parliamentary democracies and why upsets sometimes lead them to change policy, to alter their legislative calendar or to revise their thinking about the timing of general elections, even if their public posture is to dismiss them as routine, midterm reversals.[4]

But despite its widespread currency, such an interpretation of the electoral dynamic of this particular type of parliamentary contest remains at least questionable and it does so for three reasons. In the first place, not everybody, important politicians included, sets a great deal of store by it. Speaking in 1904, the then British Prime Minister, Arthur Balfour, voiced his own scepticism: 'I do not for one instant admit that by-elections are a test, or ought to be regarded as a test, of public feeling. They are, of course, a test of the feelings of a particular constituency at the time the by-election takes place. They are not, and they cannot be made, the index and the test of what the feeling of the people of the country is as a whole.'[5] In the second place, little empirical support has been found for it. One study of inter-war British by-elections concludes: 'Recapitulating the results of this survey, we can say with some definiteness that...a(s) a political barometer,...the by-election is unreliable and of little significance.'[6] Finally, the previous two chapters of this book have found little evidence for the claim of a strong national component to the short-term dynamics of by-election turnout. The long-term forces of country and partisanship apart, the local force of the marginality of the seat has proved to be the only consistent short-term influence in this type of election. This is not to deny, of course, that national public opinion could be strong enough in its impact to do what, say, candidate characteristics could not and override this localism. Equally, however, there is no readily apparent reason to take for granted that public opinion is sufficiently strong to have this effect. And even if it does, all its facets need not be equally instrumental in shaping all aspects of voting turnout patterns. The public's loyalty to the traditional Conservative, Labour and Liberal parties may be influential under certain circumstances, e.g., in general elections when class loyalties run high, and its assessment of the governing and opposition parties influential under others, e.g., in by-elections when, for some, the incumbent government is 'on trial'.

The inevitable conclusion of this debate can only be that the nature of national public opinion's electoral impact, if any, is an hypothesis that needs to be tested rather than an article of faith to be accepted without question. It is to the testing of this hypothesis, in the specific context of the determination of turnout patterns, that this chapter now turns.

National Standing of the Parties

As used herein, the phrase 'the national standing of a political party' refers to its popularity with the electorate as a whole. It is a multi-dimensional concept since there is any number of party features that can appeal, or otherwise, to potential voters. Examples that spring readily to mind are its ideology, its traditional image, its internal unity, its leaders and their character traits and, finally, its past or present performance in government. In the best of all possible worlds, sound theoretical considerations would determine which of these various dimensions of party evaluation should figure in the investigation of turnout patterns, but such a luxury is not available here. Rather, this analysis' range of choice is constrained by the data available so that the party features figuring as predictor variables in it derive from a set of questions asked by the Gallup polling organisation of nationwide samples of British electors over the 1950 to 1983 period. These questions elicit from respondents their voting intention, if any, their satisfaction with the Prime Minister, their assessment of the Opposition Leader and their approval or disapproval of the government's record to date.[7]

The measures of party standing afforded by this battery of

Table 5.1: Percentage mean and range of party standing measures by type of election

	General elections		By-elections	
Voting intention	*Mean*	*Range*	*Mean*	*Range*
Governing	47.5	40-51	41.1	27-54
Opposition	44.5	36-51	45.3	25-55
Conservative	46.7	36-51	43.6	27-55
Labour	45.3	40-51	42.9	25-54
Liberal	07.5	02-18	12.4	03-42
Don't Know	10.9	04-18	12.3	06-22
Party Leaders				
Prime Minister	56.2	43-71	47.7	13-79
Opposition	41.8	28-58	41.2	14-67
Conservative	52.0	28-71	44.7	13-79
Labour	48.7	43-60	45.2	14-67
Government Record	45.8	33-57	39.7	18-60

questions fall into three categories, the first relating to support for a party, the second to support for party leaders, and the third to the public's evalaution of the incumbent government's performance in office. Table 5.1 specifies the precise measures falling into each of the categories and presents information on their individual distributions over the 1950 to 1983 period. The general election figures are averaged over the ten months in which such elections were held and the by-election figures over the much larger number of months in which the by-elections comprising this study took place.[8] The table contains few surprises. In general terms, voting intentions can be seen to be better crystallised and their distribution more clearly centred around the Conservative and Labour parties in high-stimulus general elections. The electorate also tends to rally around its party leaders and government more in those elections where the stakes are high. What is especially noteworthy, though, is the considerably greater variation in the party leader and government approval variables compared to the voting intention ones. This difference characterises both types of election and might be taken to indicate that the electorate's evaluation of its government and party leaders is substantially independent of its party loyalties.

But care should be taken before embracing this conclusion, not least because it flies in the face of the well-documented tendency for

British electors to view the political world through highly partisan spectacles with the result that their perceptions of party leaders and government performance are shaped very substantially by their long-term party loyalty.[9] And, indeed, progressing beyond the distribution of the individual measures to look at how they relate to each other appears to confirm the primacy of party. The first indication of its structuring influence comes from an examination of the zero-order correlations between the party voting intention measures on the one hand and the party leader and government approval ones on the other. To state the matter bluntly, it is very rare for the two sets of measures to be substantially independent of each other. To take a few by-election examples, the coefficient for governing party vote and satisfaction with the Prime Minister is 0.79, for the Labour vote and Opposition leader it is 0.70, for the governing party vote and Conservative leader it is .53 and for the Labour vote and Labour leader it is 0.85.[10] On top of this government approval is correlated at a level of 0.83 with governing party vote intention and of 0.82 with satisfaction with the Prime Minister. This pattern of high inter-correlations is also found in the general election party standing variables.[11]

This pattern of relationships suggests two conclusions, one conceptual and the other statistical. The conceptual conclusion is that party does indeed seem to be the principal means by which British electors orient themselves politically, even in low-stimulus elections; leaders play a secondary role at best. The statistical conclusion is that the voting intention variables cannot be included in the same regression equation as the party leader and government approval measures because of the horrendous multicollinearity problem that would be created if they were; stable estimates of the impact of each variable would simply not be obtainable. Under these circumstances, *a priori* reasoning dictates that the voting intention group of variables should constitute the basis of the analysis to follow. The dominant role played by party loyalty in the British electorate leaves no other choice. Precautions can be taken, however, to ensure that the forced exclusion of the other measures of party standing does not lead to the sacrifice of valuable information regarding the role of party leaders in determining turnout patterns and these precautions involve the repetition of all the analyses with the party leader variables included in place of their collinear voting intention counterparts. This exercise was carried out, but, apart from a few footnotes, its results are not reported herein since the leader variables usually perform worse as predictors of both the level and rate of change of turnout. Just as it has been elsewhere with party choice, in other words, this analysis confirms the primary structuring role of party with regard to the second dimension of the voting act, electoral participation.

Level of Turnout

The preceding discussion has served to define the broad parameters of this chapter's analysis of the relationship between the national standing of the parties and turnout patterns in general and by-elections. In addition to the usual long-term forces of partisanship and country, the predictor variables figuring in the following cross-sectional regression analyses will comprise the proportion of the electorate expressing an intention to vote for the governing, opposition, Conservative, Labour and Liberal parties, as well as the proportion responding 'don't know' when asked their current voting intention. Two minor modifications remain to be made to this list, however. The first concerns the measure of popular support for the government. There are two candidates for this role, governing party voting intention and government approval. Both measures cannot be used since they are correlated at a value of 0.91 in general elections and 0.82 in by-elections and two considerations dictate that the approval variable be chosen. The first is that by-election outcomes are commonly interpreted as referenda on the incumbent government's peformance in office and a direct measure of the public's approval of this performance would seem to offer a more valid and sensitive test of this hypothesis than its more stable and resilient counterpart, governing party vote intention. The second consideration is the straightforwardly empirical one that approval does in fact perform better than voting intention in the sense of having greater substantive importance, especially in the explanation of turnout change.

The second modification is the inclusion in the list of predictors of the electoral marginality variable. As in the last chapter, this variable is included for sound theoretical reasons and not just for its likely simplifying effect on the pattern of results. Marginality is, after all, a constituency characteristic that could profoundly mediate the influence of the parties' standing in the nation at large so that not to take it into account runs the very real risk of producing an exaggerated estimate of its importance for turnout. Growing disapproval of government performance, for example, might be uniform across Britain and, other things being equal, serve to depress by-election turnout to the same degree in all constituencies. Taking note of the national situation, however, well-organised parties in marginal government seats especially might well make a special effort to mobilise by-election support and thereby mitigate the size of the drop in turnout levels that could have been expected in view of the government's falling popularity. Reliable estimates of the relative impact of the parties' national standing, therefore, require that marginality be included in the analyses to come.

Table 5.2: Standardised coefficients for the regression of turnout on the party standing variables by type of election

	General election turnout			By-election turnout	
(.38)	% Conservative	0.46	(.30)	Marginality	0.32
(.32)	Marginality	0.37	(.23)	Country	0.27
(.01)	% Labour	0.17	(.21)	Partisanship	0.21
(.07)	Country	0.13		$R^2 = 20.0$	
	$R^2 = 28.7$				

Table 5.2 presents the results of regressing turnout levels in the two types of election on marginality, partisanship, country, opposition, Conservative, Labour, Liberal and don't know voting intention and government approval; the variables figuring in the table have satisfied the criterion of having a regression coefficient that is twice the size of its standard error or greater. Thus, taking general election turnout first, Table 5.2 can be seen to have two salient features. The first is that turnout in this type of parliamentary election is higher when the Conservative and Labour parties, and especially the former, enjoy greater popularity in the country as a whole. That is, it is traditional party loyalties rather than more immediate assessments of the governing and opposition parties, that mobilise electors in general elections. This finding is important because it enhances the credibility of Chapter 3's speculation as to the depressant effect on general election turnout of the post-1966 erosion of these loyalties, as reflected in the growth in the number of candidatures per constituency in this period. The greater mobilisation power enjoyed by Conservative party popularity is probably to some extent a function of an argument

also first articulated in Chapter 3 and cropping up again in Chapter 4, namely that its supporters tend to be somewhat more politically aware and responsive than their Labour counterparts and thus more likely to take the trouble to cast their ballot, especially, it would seem, when the stakes in the election are high and their party is riding high in the polls. Alternatively, of course, it might be that what we have here is simply a bandwagon effect and Conservative supporters, being more deferential to their party, are the more likely to be mindlessly carried along by the ups and downs in its fortunes. This latter interpretation of the relationship is not very convincing, however, since, coming disproportionately from the middle class, Conservative supporters will generally score higher on attributes like education and political interest and information that will help to make their electoral response to their political environment anything but mindless or devoid of calculated self-interest.[12]

Table 5.2's second salient feature with regard to general election turnout is marginality's secondary explanatory role. Again, this is not altogether surprising or difficult to explain since the organisational mobilisation of the vote is only one of several powerful stimuli getting voters to the polls in elections of this type. Indeed, to look at the finding positively, marginality's subordination to Conservative popularity is the strongest evidence yet for the national character of the general election turnout dynamic; other indicators of it, like the candidate number variable in Chapter 3, apply only to specific groups of seats, whereas this one applies across the board.

By-election turnout is another story altogether. Insofar as none of the party standing variables has a significant effect on it, it once again shows itself to be impervious to the influence of short-term political forces. As in Chapter 3, the impression that is given is that, at least with regard to their turnout levels, by-elections are entirely introverted events into which the outside world does not intrude. Their stimulus level would seem to be so low that the electorate does not link them with the national political process and is prodded to turn out to vote only by the mobilisation efforts of local political parties and by tradition and habit, as represented by the long-term forces of country and partisanship. National short-term forces in particular, whether they emanate from the political context or from the standing of the parties themselves, are largely irrelevant to any understanding of by-election turnout. Nor can their irrelevance be dismissed as an artefact of their 'real' effect being neutralised by party effort in the more competitive seats. To re-run the by-election equation in Table 5.2 without the marginality variable does not allow any of the party standing variables to emerge as significant predictors; its only effect is to reduce the overall explanatory power of the equation.[13]

The final observation to be made on Table 5.2 concerns the absence from it of either a general or by-election effect for the government approval and opposition voting intention variables. Where public feelings towards the parties influence turnout, it is its traditional party loyalties rather than its immediate evaluations of the government and opposition that do so.[14] But precipitate conclusions should be avoided since it could well be that they will prove premature. Chapter 4 has demonstrated that only the incumbent candidate has an effect on constituency turnout patterns so it seems reasonable to hypothesise that each party's standing in national public opinion will have a turnout effect only in those seats that it holds. The testing of this hypothesis involves the introduction into the analysis of the party incumbency variable, first in its Conservative and Labour form and then its government and opposition one. Previous chapters have demonstrated that the interaction of the incumbency, marginality and other predictor variables provides a uniform set of results across neither turnout dimensions nor groups of seats and this chapter promises to reiterate this complexity, not least because the early indications are that the national party standing variables may be a potent influence on general election turnout, but they do not have this effect in by-elections.

The immediate impression to be gained from comparing Conservative- and Labour-held seats in Table 5.3 is that the promise of complexity has been kept in its entirety. Being uniformly preeminent across neither type of election nor seat groupings, the unprecedentedly variable role of marginality is especially striking. In one sense, of course, this variability is easily explained; it is a general testament to the explanatory potency of the party popularity variables. But it is the conditions under which these are more or less potent that is the more informative, and interesting, feature of the table.

To take general election turnout first, there are very clear differences between the regression outcomes in Conservative and Labour seats and these are not easily understood at first glance. The problem does not lie with the Conservative equation since its outcome is perfectly consonant with previous findings and speculation as to their meaning. The seat's competitiveness has

Table 5.3: Standardised coefficients for the regression of turnout on the party standing variables by Conservative and Labour incumbency and type of election

General election turnout

	Conservative incumbency			*Labour incumbency*	
(.49)	Marginality	0.53	(.43)	% Don't know	0.42
(.27)	% Conservative	0.29	(-.44)	% Liberal	-0.30
	$R^2 = 33.6$		(.13)	% Govt. Approval	-0.30
			(.20)	Marginality	0.26
			(.19)	Country	0.24
				$R^2 = 37.3$	

By-election turnout

	Conservative incumbency			*Labour incumbency*	
(-.44)	% Conservative	-0.47	(.32)	Marginality	0.39
(.26)	Marginality	0.30	(.26)	Country	0.34
(.30)	Partisanship	0.25		$R^2 = 21.3$	
	$R^2 = 33.6$				

always been the preeminent predictor of general election turnout in Conservative seats and its primacy is in all likelihood a reflection of that party's organisational superiority, a superiority that is itself grounded in a full recognition that loss or victory in British general elections hinges on the way in which a relatively small number of marginal constituencies swing rather than on patterns of stasis and change in the full panoply of them.[15] The purpose of party organisation thus becomes to ensure a favourable outcome in the party's more marginal seats through the fullest possible mobilisation of those social groups likely to cast their ballot for the party. A second source of voter mobilisation in Conservative seats proves to be the relatively intangible one of the party's national standing. Assuming for the moment that it is Conservative supporters who are more likely to make their way to the polls when the party is popular, its positive effect reinforces earlier speculation about Conservative constituency electorates being generally more aware of, and responsive to, their political environment. In this regard, it is noticeable that the Labour party's popularity does not even figure in the second general election equation.

More generally, though, it is impossible to interpret the Labour incumbency equation without resorting to a great deal of convoluted and largely unconvincing reasoning. It is difficult, for example, to see why high levels of national uncertaintly about which party to vote for should increase turnout at all; the reverse could more reasonably be expected. The basic problem is that the pattern of results is a statistical artefact arising from inability of any single predictor variable to exercise a sufficiently decisive impact on the dependent variable to produce a clear solution and a comparison with the the correlation coefficients for the significant predictors in Conservative seats throws this difference into sharp relief. The result is that small differences in the value of the correlation coefficients in Labour seats determine the order in which the individual variables are entered into the stepwise regression analysis and an unclear, somewhat arbitrary solution is the outcome.[16] For this reason, it is probably wiser to focus on what this outcome does not say rather than what it does say. In other words, Labour seats are most noteworthy for the failure of either marginality or the party's standing in the country as a whole decisively to influence the level of general election turnout in them. The overall impression, therefore, is once again of a political party that has relatively little control of its political environment. The mobilisation of its support in even its less safe seats is largely out of its hands, regardless of whether or not the party itself is popular nationally or partisanship is running high in the electorate. In short, the Labour party suffers not only from poor organisation, but also, it would appear, from having a group of supporters who generally have neither the same sense of self-interest as their Conservative counterparts nor the same readiness to take to the polls to defend it when the prize is the control of government.

The distinctiveness of the regression outcome in each group of seats is equally apparent in by-elections, largely because of the failure of any of the party standing variables to influence their turnout levels in Labour seats. The popularity of the incumbent party is, on the other hand, the clearly preeminent predictor in Conservative seats. But far more unexpected and interesting is that its by-election influence is negative in direction. Thus, the Conservative party's national standing may boost general election turnout in the seats that it controls, but it has the opposite effect on by-election turnout and the very fact of its being negatively signed means that the variable's powerful effect cannot be 'explained away' in terms of something like the parties' lower level of organisational preparedness to fight by-elections. After all, even if it were the case that their organisation is always less finely honed in by-elections, which is by no means necessarily so, the most this would help to explain is why the national force of party standing comes to the explanatory fore; it casts no light at all on why it is negatively signed in its prominence.

There is a relatively simple and plausible explanation, however, and it is that supporter complacency is the price that the Conservative party pays at by-elections for national popularity, even in its more marginal seats. Albeit for different reasons, this complacency may well affect the supporters of all parties in Conservative-held seats, but Table 5.3 suggests two reasons for believing that it is disproportionately concentrated among the incumbent party's own supporters. The first is that if it were an effect common to the supporters of all parties, then Labour party popularity could reasonably be expected to have a similar effect in Labour seats and, indeed, in Conservative ones as well. It has an effect in neither grouping, though. The second, and directly related, reason lies in the party popularity variable's differential importance in the two groups of seats. A conclusion the analysis in this book has suggested repeatedly is that Conservative supporters respond more sensitively to their political environment than do Labour supporters. This being the case, the far more powerful explanatory role for the party popularity variable in Conservative seats can be interpreted as yet one more manifestation of this greater sensitivity. When the Conservative party is unpopular nationally, by-election support in all its seats is more readily mobilised because the threat of defeat looms larger. But when the party is popular, complacency afflicts its supporters in even in its more marginal seats.[17]

Two conclusions follow from Table 5.3, then. The first is that both general and by-election turnout levels in Conservative as opposed to Labour seats differ markedly in their susceptibility to being influenced by how their incumbent party stands in the public opinion polls. Moreover, there are two reasons why this difference cannot be attributed to organisational discrepancies in the two seat groupings. On the one hand, the difference persists strongly even after the marginality of the seat is controlled. On the other hand, if it were organisational weakness that allowed the popularity variables to emerge as significant predictors, these variables could be expected to figure more prominently in Labour seats since it is in these that party organisation is generally weaker. As it is, however, these variables are more prominent in Conservative seats. In all likelihood, therefore, their different impact reflects qualitative differences in the stimuli to which constituency electorates react, with the evidence indicating that those in Conservative seats are far more sensitive and responsive to their national political environment than those in Labour ones. The second conclusion rests on the observation that, just as with general and by-elections as a whole, such party standing variables as do have an influence in Conservative seats are not related to popular evaluations of government performance.[18] Thus the hypothesis that by-election turnout in particular is shaped by the popular standing of the government at the time of the election can only be rejected for want of supporting evidence. With this conclusion holding equally for general elections, there is simply no evidence to support this hypothesis. Indeed, the only way in which the hypothesis might be salvaged is to refine it so that it is held to apply only in the restricted context of government and opposition seats. It is to the the investigation of this possibility that this analysis now turns.

Table 5.4: Standardised coefficients for the regression of turnout on the party standing variables by government and opposition incumbency and type of election

General election turnout

	Government incumbency			*Opposition incumbency*	
(.45)	% Conservative	0.57	(.23)	Marginality	0.30
(.37)	Marginality	0.39	(.25)	% Conservative	0.29
(.06)	% Labour	0.24		$R^2=13.3$	
(.07)	Country	0.14			
	$R^2=37.9$				

By-election turnout

	Government incumbency			*Opposition incumbency*	
(-.33)	% Conservative	-0.47	(.38)	Marginality	0.42
(.26)	Marginality	0.28	(.19)	Country	0.23
(.24)	Country	0.28	(.23)	Partisanship	0.21
(-.28)	% Labour	-0.28		$R^2=24.9$	
(-.04)	% Opposition	0.27			
(.20)	Partisanship	0.21			
	$R^2=30.3$				

Party popularity's effect on turnout levels in government and opposition seats is summarised in Table 5.4. It is plainly evident, first, that the systematic differences are more between government and opposition seats and less between types of election and, second, that the principal reason for this pattern of differences is the general irrelevance of party standing to the explanation of either general or by-election turnout levels in opposition seats. The one exception is Conservative popularity's general election effect in these seats, but not too much should be made of this relationship. In the first place, since it simply reiterates the earlier demonstrated importance of Conservative party popularity for turnout in this type of election generally, there is nothing distinctive about this relationship inhering in opposition as compared with government seats. In the second place, the relatively low level of variance explained by the equation as a whole indicates that it is not a strong relationship. Finally, bearing at least as convincing witness to party standing's essential unimportance in opposition seats is consideration of the argument that this phenomenon's 'true' importance is masked by the overriding importance for turnout of the competitiveness of the seat. If this argument were valid, to exclude marginality should bring at least one or two of the popularity measures into the picture as significant predictors of turnout in one or both of general and by-elections, but it does no such thing. Instead, all that happens is that, marginality apart, exactly the same variables comprise the two equations and their overall explanatory power is reduced.[19]

The general impression left by this discussion is once again that parliamentary elections in opposition seats unfold in a short-term political vacuum. Perhaps because little is at stake in these seats in the sense that elections in them do not afford the opportunity to censure the government, never mind throw it out of office, their constituency electorates seem relatively insensitive to, and unmoved by, aspects of their short-term political environment other than the local organisational mobilisation of the vote. But at the same time that turnout levels in these seats are unaffected by government popularity, they are equally unmoved by the national standing of the opposition party. Indeed, this party's popularity has a little more of an impact in government seats where it boosts by-election turnout. Thus, the adversarial model that sees the moving force in British elections to be the perennial struggle between government and opposition parties for voter's affections and support seems, to say the least, overdrawn in its characterisation of the mobilisation of the parliamentary election vote. It is not even as if the governing party's popularity is a significant influence on this aspect of the voting act in the restricted context of government seats.[20]

Excluding the marginality variable has no effect on the general election equations in Table 5.4; Conservative and Labour voting intention become the only two significant predictors in government seats and Conservative voting intention the only one in opposition seats. The same exercise with by-elections produces more interesting results, however. Country and partisanship remain the only influences in opposition seats, but government approval, with a beta weight of -0.25, displaces the Labour and opposition voting intention variables in government seats.[21] Most noticeable about government approval's effect is that, like its Conservative and Labour counterparts, it is negative and all three relationships emphasise the role played by elector complacency in the structuring of by-election turnout. The most likely explanation of complacency's importance is that, relatively little being at stake in by-elections, they are less adversarial than general elections and party propaganda and the felt need to go to the polls consequently less urgent. Complacency may thus be seen as both cause and consequence of the generally low-stimulus character of this type of parliamentary election. But this complacency is not necessarily determinative. As Table 5.4 shows, once the competitiveness of the seat is taken into account, government approval's negative effect in government-held seats recedes into insignificance. It seems that the governing party's determination to get out its vote so as not to risk a humiliating by-election defeat overcomes the complacency of its would-be supporters.

To sum up, then, this chapter's analysis of the relationship between national party standing and general and by-election turnout levels has suggested two important conclusions. The first of them concerns the conventional wisdom as to the predominantly national dynamic underpinning stasis and change in the pattern of British electoral politics. Chapters 3 and 4 of this book have already indicated that, insofar as it is profoundly mediated in both types of parliamentary election by the constituency characteristics of marginality and party incumbency, the national character of this dynamic has been exaggerated - at least for voting turnout. The degree of its exaggeration, furthermore, has been shown to be far greater for by-elections than for general elections, the former repeatedly having been demonstrated to be largely immune to the impact of short-term political forces of either the national or local variety. Confronting this distinction with its first direct measures of national party popularity, the purpose of this chapter was in part to put it to the systematic test.

The first conclusion to emerge from this exercise is that the differences that there are between the general and by-election turnout dynamics are of degree rather than kind. Taking Tables 5.2, 5.3 and 5.4 together, both dynamics can be characterised as local insofar as the marginality variable figures in all ten equations and is preeminent in two of the five general election ones and three of the five by-election ones. Equally, both are national in the sense that neither is free of influence from the party popularity variables; one or more of these variables appears in all five general election equations, but in only two of the five by-election ones. This is the only unambiguous evidence in Chapters 3, 4 and 5 of a by-election effect for short-term political forces, but it is an effect that does not make itself felt across the board. The distinction between the two types of election is blurred by the effect of the second constituency characteristic, party incumbency. The party standing variables, and especially popular support for the Conservative party, play a prominent explanatory role in Conservative and government seats and not in Labour and opposition ones. The electorates in these last two seat groupings just do not seem as responsive to their short-term political environment.

The observation that the individual party standing variables perform differently in different seat groupings is the stimulus for the second conclusion to be drawn from the chapter up to this point. When the standing variables are influential, both general and by-election turnout levels are always more responsive to the strength of traditional party loyalties in the electorate than they are to popular assessments of the relative merits of the governing and opposition parties. Once again, this conclusion is truer of general than by-elections. Indeed, it is only on by-election turnout in government seats that the government popularity variable can be argued to have any effect at all. But even here the substantive significance of its impact is easily exaggerated and is certainly neither pervasive nor dominant enough to vindicate the argument that popular feelings about the government's performance is the principal force structuring electoral behaviour in either type of election. On reflection, though, perhaps it is unreasonable even to hope for its vindication since it may be that this hypothesis is more accurately framed not in terms of the absolute level of government popularity, but of trends in this popularity from the time of the government's assumption of office. This being the case, it is changing levels of government popularity that can be expected to influence the pattern of turnout change. This refined hypothesis will now be tested.

Rate of Change of Turnout

As in the previous two chapters, there proves to be an unavoidable discrepancy between the optimum and the feasible in terms of the range of predictor variables that can be used in the investigation of the determinants of turnout change. The optimum set of variables would comprise those used in the preceding cross-sectional analysis plus, where applicable, the change measures on these same variables. But what is optimum in conceptual terms, turns out not to be feasible in statistical terms since the cross-sectional and change versions of the party standing variables are highly intercorrelated, causing the multicollinearity problem to rear its ugly head once again. The nature of the problem can be gauged from an examination of the inter-version simple correlations; these are 0.79 for Conservative popularity, 0.90 for Labour popularity, 0.71 for Liberal popularity, 0.82 for opposition party popularity, 0.17 for don't know voting intention and 0.71 for government approval.[22] The magnitude of these coefficients means that, with the exception of don't know voting intention, only one or other version of the party standing variables can be included in the analysis of turnout change. Fortunately, the choice between them is not a difficult one to make since the theoretical thrust of this section of the chapter is the relationship between trends, or change, in the national standing of the parties and the rate of change of turnout between parliamentary elections. The included variables are, therefore, marginality, country, partisanship, don't know voting intention and change on the marginality, partisanship, Conservative, Labour, Liberal, opposition, don't know voting intention and government approval variables.[23]

The determinants of turnout change for the full population of constituencies are presented in Table 5.5. It is immediately noticeable that, unlike in Chapters 3 and 4, two sets of results are reported; these are the regression outcomes including and excluding the marginality variables. The reason for this departure from past practice is the very good one that, unlike in either previous chapters or the previous section of this one, the decision as to whether to include or exclude the marginality variables has a profound substantive importance for the conclusions to be drawn from this section. This will become apparent as the interpretation of the tables proceeds.

Table 5.5: Standardised coefficients for the regression of turnout change on the party standing variables[*]

	Inter-election turnout change				
	Inc. marginality			*Exc. marginality*	
(-.36)	Δ Marginality	-0.51	(-.17)	Δ % Govt. approval	-0.26
(-.17)	Marginality	-0.42	(-.25)	Country	-0.24
(.16)	Δ Partisanship	0.26	(-.05)	Δ % Opposition	-0.14
(-.25)	Country	-0.24		$R^2 = 10.7$	
(-.13)	Δ % Liberal	-0.24			
	$R^2 = 38.1$				

[*]Δ denotes change

When the full panoply of predictor variables is included, the results are perfectly consonant with those of earlier chapters insofar as they show the turnout change dynamic to be predominantly local in inspiration. After all, the two versions of the marginality variable are clearly the most powerful predictors. But with changing partisanship and country coming next, short-term forces relating to party popularity are not very prominent. Change in Liberal popularity is the only party standing variable to figure in the equation and it is the last-ranked predictor. As voting support for it increases, the drop in turnout gets smaller, probably reflecting a tendency for a number of disgruntled major party supporters to express a voting intention for it in preference to the other major party or abstention. But its continuity with previous results notwithstanding, the more remarkable feature of the configuration of results in Table 5.5 is the absence from it of any impact for changing evaluations of government performance. This variable's failure to emerge as a significant predictor would suggest that the referendum hypothesis has as little validity in the explanation of turnout change as it does in that of turnout levels.

In one sense, of course, this conclusion has to be accepted; all things considered and across all constituencies, this analysis indicates that changing evaluations of government performance have not affected the pattern of turnout change in British parliamentary elections. But to leave the matter there does not explain why, contrary to popular mythology, they have not. Is it simply that this national force has no effect under any circumstances or is it that its effect is overshadowed by some more powerful predictor? If the latter option offers the solution to the puzzle, the most likely candidate for the role of suppressor variable is the competitiveness of the seat. It has already been argued that party organisations ready themselves for an election with an eye to its anticipated outcome rather than to past outcomes in the same constituency. This being the case, parties in the more marginal seats are likely to make a special effort to mobilise by-election support when the government is unpopular; the governing party to try to offset the adverse consequences of its growing unpopularity and the opposition party to take advantage of it. Under these circumstances, the closeness of a contest could well be expected to relegate changing government popularity to the realm of the inconsequential in the explanation of turnout change. According to this hypothesis, then, were marginality not controlled, changing levels of government popularity should exercise some influence on the turnout decline that almost inevitably accompanies the transition from general to by-elections, which is indeed what it does (see Table 5.5). To discount marginality serves to elevate the opposition party variable to a position of explanatory prominence as well. But what is especially interesting about its presence is less its moderating effect on turnout decline and more its confirmation that the public's assessment of the opposition, as well as the governing, party does, under certain conditions, play a significant role in shaping turnout patterns in Britain's Conservative- and Labour-dominated party system.[24] These conditions, however, involve the rather unrealistic discounting of the important mediating effect of the marginality of the seat and the disproportionate mobilisation effort that a close contest entails.

Table 5.5 has, of course, demonstrated that this assessment plays no significant role when all by-election constituencies are considered together and their marginality is controlled. But it could well be that this picture will change if the second local characteristic of demonstrated importance, party incumbency, is also taken into account. It might be, for example, that changing traditional party loyalties will play the dominant role in Conservative and Labour seats, whereas this role will belong to changing governing and opposition party loyalties in government and opposition seats. In keeping with past practice, Conservative and Labour seats will be compared first.

Table 5.6: Standardised coefficients for the regression of turnout change on the party standing variables by Conservative and Labour incumbency and type of election[*]

Conservative incumbency

	Inc. marginality			*Exc. marginality*	
(-.41)	Δ Marginality	-0.59	(-.40)	Δ % Liberal	-0.77
(-.25)	Δ % Govt. approval	-0.37	(-.04)	Δ % Labour	-0.48
(-.09)	Marginality	-0.26	(.10)	Δ Partisanship	0.47
(-.24)	Country	-0.18	(-.24)	Country	-0.17
	R^2=37.9			R^2=32.8	

Labour Incumbency

	Inc. marginality			*Exc. marginality*	
(-.34)	Δ Marginality	-0.55	(-.22)	Country	-0.24
(-.21)	Marginality	-0.54	(-.26)	Δ % Conservative	-0.19
(-.22)	Country	-0.26		R^2=12.4	
	R^2=37.2				

[*] Δ denotes change

Whether or not the effect of marginality is controlled, Table 5.6 in fact confirms that there is little consistent support for the hypothesis of a dominant government-opposition dialectic in the explanation of turnout change. On the whole, the explanatory power of inter-election change in support for the traditional parties is more in evidence. Taking for granted marginality's pre-eminence when included in the equation, the striking feature of the table is the different role played by the party standing variables in the two groups of seats. These variables barely influence turnout change in Labour seats whether or not their marginality is taken into account. But the picture is very different in Conservative seats where changing party evaluations can be seen to play a prominent explanatory role whether or not the marginality of the individual constituencies is controlled. As hypothesised on a number of occasions previously, this difference suggests the existence of a generally more aware and responsive electorate in Conservative seats. There, to exclude the marginality variables allows the growth of support for the Labour and especially Liberal parties to attenuate turnout decline. The Liberal relationship suggests once again that Conservative supporters are more likely to express their dissatisfaction with their party (which may be in government as well as incumbent in the constituency) not by abstaining or riskily switching their support to the other major party, but by switching it, albeit temporarily perhaps, to the Liberal party. Presumably, however, this practice of 'tactical switching' is disproportionately common in competitive Conservative seats because when their marginality is taken into account, changing Liberal party support ceases to influence the rate of change of turnout, its place being taken by inter-election change in the level of government approval. Mobilisational effort, in other words, may offset the tendency for growing Liberal party support to reduce the magnitude of turnout decline, and presumably its exacerbation of the Conservative party's vote losses, but its other consequence is to make government performance a by-election issue in Conservative seats. Taken together with the observation that, unlike in the cross-sectional equations in Table 5.3, the Conservative party's own national standing has no effect on turnout change in Table 5.5, this finding suggests that traditional party loyalties are not the dominant influence on all three turnout dimensions. They may be less influential in structuring the rate of change of turnout, as opposed to its level, precisely because by-election abstention is more a reaction to how the more aware public in Conservative seats feels, albeit transiently, about the incumbent government's performance and less to how it feels in midterm about the party to which it feels a more enduring attachment.[25]

More generally, though, perhaps not too much should be made of government approval's importance. After all, it figures in Conservative seats, but not in Labour ones. In addition, there is no explanatory role for changes in the opposition party's popularity in either group of seats. A government-opposition dialectic can hardly be held, therefore, to be a driving force behind turnout change in either or both of Conservative and Labour seats. Importantly, however, changing traditional party loyalties assume this role even less convincingly when marginality is controlled. But if electors do respond to the party incumbent in their constituency less in terms of its traditional image and more in terms of whether or not it is currently in government, it is not at all surprising that to compare Conservative and Labour seats fails to produce a well-defined picture. This formulation does, after all, compound the two parties' periods in and out of government. A clearer picture may emerge when government and opposition seats are compared.

Table 5.7: Standardised coefficients for the regression of turnout change on the party standing variables by government and opposition incumbency and type of election[*]

Government incumbency

	Inc. marginality			*Exc. marginality*	
(-.29)	Δ Marginality	-0.41	(-.34)	Δ % Govt. approval	-0.42
(-.06)	Marginality	-0.36	(-.02)	Δ % Conservative	-0.33
(-.30)	Country	-0.30	(-.30)	Country	-0.26
(-.34)	Δ % Govt. approval	-0.29	(.09)	% Don't know	0.25
(-.02)	Δ % Conservative	-0.24	(.01)	Δ % Don't know	0.16
	R^2=32.3			R^2=25.3	

Opposition incumbency

	Inc. marginality			*Exc. marginality*	
(-.30)	Δ Marginality	-0.64		Not significant	
(-.36)	Marginality	-0.53			
(-.03)	Δ % Govt. approval	-0.24			
	R^2=35.4				

[*] Δ denotes change

These two groups of seats are compared in Table 5.7 and it does indeed make for a more decisive and coherent picture of the dynamics of turnout change than is to be found in Table 5.6's comparison of Conservative and Labour seats, the major difference being that change in the governing party's popularity plays an explanatory role in both government and opposition seats. Before examining this role in some detail, however, it is worth noting that changing patterns of support for the opposition party do not figure in Table 5.7 at all despite being given every chance to do so. Their absence only serves to confirm the earlier conclusion as to the essential irrelevance to an understanding of turnout patterns in British parliamentary elections of the notion of a proselytising opposition that, offering itself as a credible alternative government, represents a continuous threat to the party already in power.

Whether or not its popularity increases from general to by-election, the evidence throughout this book indicates that the British electors are blind to the opposition party, even in the constituencies it controls. The adversarial interpretation of the British electorate's response to the parties must, therefore, be seriously qualified.

Adversarial politics may not inform the pattern of turnout change in government and opposition seats, but anti-government sentiment certainly does so and, when marginality is excluded, its effect is stronger than any other variable's in those seats held by the government.[26] The decrease in popularity that almost inevitably besets governments is the most potent predictor of turnout change in them and the bigger it gets, the more it moderates turnout decline, presumably as the governing party makes a special effort to offset its growing unpopularity and the opposition a special effort to take advantage of it. The other party standing standing variable to have the same effect is Conservative party popularity. Even if secondary, its strength in the government incumbency equation excluding marginality serves as a salutary reminder of the motive power of traditional party loyalties, especially those relating to the Conservative party, in the British electorate. But not too much should be read into these relativities for the moment. After all, the equation from which they are derived takes no account of previous indications that, across the whole range of constituencies, marginality overshadows the decline in government popularity's in its impact on turnout change seats (see Table 5.5). In other words, if their relative importance in the real world of elections is to be established with any degree of confidence, the constituency characteristic of marginality needs to be controlled.

Rather unexpectedly perhaps, Table 5.7 shows that the inclusion of the marginality variables makes for a different pattern of results in opposition seats, but not in government ones. On the one hand, to control for parties' organisational mobilisation of the vote allows changing government popularity to emerge as a significant, if relatively weak, predictor in seats where the opposition party is incumbent. Its effect is to moderate turnout decline and it may reflect the efforts of the governing party to enhance its own credibility in face of its declining popularity by unexpectedly capturing an opposition seat or simply by 'putting up a good show' in by-elections. A complementary, perhaps alternative, explanation may be that opposition supporters are more readily mobilised by the governing party's misfortunes than by their own party's standing in the polls. A sound by-election defeat is certainly one way of 'teaching the rascals a lesson'. On the other hand, the marginality variables do not fundamentally alter the pattern of results in the government incumbency equation. Their only real effect is to make for the disappearance of the tendency for voter uncertainty to make the drop in turnout between general and by-election worse. Nor is this unexpected. Since getting potential and uncommitted supporters to the polls is a primary function of the organisational mobilisation of the vote, party effort would seem to pay handsome dividends in government seats.

Of more general interest, though is that it is not equal to the task of neutralising the turnout effect of changes over time in the public's evaluation of the government's performance. As was the case in Conservative and Labour seats (see Table 5.6), this variable is more powerful than matching change in support for any of the Conservative, Labour and Liberal parties once the marginality variables are taken into account. Thus, while an anti-government reaction may have little influence on the level of general and by-election turnout, it more strongly informs the rate of change of turnout in Conservative and government seats than does inter-election change in the level of support for the traditional parties.

Conclusion

This chapter's examination of the turnout effect of stasis and change in popular support for Britain's major parties leads to a set of conclusions that contain a mixture of the by now familiar and, attesting to the potency of the party standing variables, the new. The familiar concerns the contribution of short-term national forces (as opposed to the local one of marginality) to the explanation of each of the three turnout dynamics. Taking these forces as a whole and not differentiating between them for the moment, they can once again be seen to be at their strongest in general elections; at least one party standing variable is to be found in each of the five general election equations and is the preeminent predictor in three of them. They are at their weakest, in contrast, in the explanation of by-election turnout. Here, marginality is the preeminent predictor in three of the five equations and short-term national forces have an effect in two of them. Inter-election turnout change is to be found between these two extremes. The seat's becoming more marginal is the first-ranked predictor in all five equations and one or more of the party standing variables is to be found in four of them. By-election turnout, then, is the least sensitive of all three to the influence of short-term political forces; it is also less sensitive than turnout change to the impact of one or other version of the marginality variable. Even its localism , in other words, is less in evidence than it has been in the previous two chapters.

The more interesting, and novel, conclusion is that the effect of the short-term forces under consideration differs less across turnout dimensions and more across type of seat. The Conservative party's popularity, for example, influences, if in contrasting directions, both general and by-election turnout in seats where it or the government is incumbent; it is joined by support for the Labour party in government seats. National forces, in contrast, affect only general election turnout in Labour and opposition seats. Similarly, the effect of these forces on the rate of change of turnout is felt strongly in Conservative and government seats and relatively weakly, if at all, in Labour and opposition ones. The crux of the difference appears to be that, for whatever reason, electorates in the latter seat groupings are not as sensitive to their national political environment so the closeness of the contest meets with little or no resistance from this environment in structuring turnout patterns. The larger importance of this observation is that it represents the strongest evidence yet for being wary of generalisations vaunting the nationalisation of British electoral politics. Even in general elections, the turnout effect of the national party standing variables is nowhere near uniform across different types of seat. To the extent that these forces have an influence, it is more uniform across turnout dimensions precisely because it is mediated by apparently enduring differences in constituency electorates' receptivity to them.

This is not to argue, though, that it is the same party standing variables that influence each turnout dimension. The situation is more complex than this. What can be said is that when party loyalties do have an effect on patterns of constituency turnout, on the whole it is loyalty to the traditional parties rather than more immediate evaluations of the government and opposition that structure turnout patterns. This is especially true in the context of general and by-election turnout where the popularity of the Conservative party is a particularly potent explanatory variable. When it comes to the rate of change of turnout, however, a somewhat different picture emerges insofar as its dynamic is fuelled predominantly by change in the public's satisfaction with the government's record in office. In opposition seats, this is the only short-term standing variable to have an effect, whereas it has a stronger effect than its Conservative party counterpart in government seats. But being restricted to the explanantion of turnout change, care should be taken not to exaggerate the extent to which the growth of anti-government feeling structures constituency turnout patterns in Britain.

Support for the Conservative party enjoys a far more pervasive explanatory role, being especially prominent in the general and by-election equations in both Conservative and government seats. Indeed, a perusal of this chapter's results bring to mind the 'hyperactive Republicans' whose existence has been graphically brought to light in the United States. These are Republican supporters whose conservative political beliefs, it is argued, lead them to participate in politics at a far greater rate than Democrats with the same strength of party identification and level of socioeconomic status.[27] Now assuming that this group has its counterpart among Conservative supporters in Britain and that it is they who are primarily responsible for the relationship between the party's popularity and turnout patterns, the interesting question that raises itself is why should these beliefs encourage participation in general elections but not in by-elections? One possible answer to this question is that high levels of political activity are less the direct product of conservative political beliefs and more that of a desire to see government policies that are best consonant with these beliefs and at worst not hostile to them. This is a particularly arduous and unremitting task when, as in recent times, much of the ideology of conservatism is unfashionable. It may be, therefore, that committed conservatives have developed an 'underdog' mentality that most influences behaviour in general elections precisely because at stake in them is control of the governing apparatus for a set period. In by-elections, in contrast, the costs of victory or defeat are not nearly so high and underdogs can afford to lower their guard and let events take their course. Even a defeat for their party is most unlikely to upset the balance of parliamentary power or deflect the government from its chosen path. Complacency on the part of the hyperactive, therefore, is a perfectly reasonable response to their party's standing high in the opinion polls at by-election time.

Notes

[1]David Butler and Donald Stokes, *Political Change in Britain*, 2nd ed. (London: Macmillan, 1974), p. 351.

[2]Dennis Kavanagh, *Constituency Electioneering in Britain* (London: Longmans, 1970), p. 28. A more rigorous demonstration of the 'nationalisation' of both turnout and voting patterns in British general elections is Donald Stokes,'Parties and the Nationalization of Electoral Forces' in Walter Dean Burnham and William N. Chambers, eds, *The American Party Systems: Stages of Development* (Oxford: Oxford University Press, 1967), 182-202. It is worth reiterating at this point that while statements like this are obviously intended to refer to voting patterns, turnout and the vote are so closely related that they can legitimately be taken to imply a turnout effect as well.

[3]Quoted in James K. Pollock, 'British By-Elections Between the Wars', *American Political Science Review*, 35 (1941), p. 519.

[4]The outcome of the 1933 East Fulham by-election, for example, may have been instrumental in delaying Britain's rearmament programme. See Martin Ceadel, 'Interpreting East Fulham' in Chris Cook and John Ramsden, eds, *By-Elections in British Politics* (London: Macmillan, 1973), 118-39. In Canada, adverse by-election outcomes have had a number of effects, ranging from the replacement of party leaders to the introduction of new policies. See R. MacGregor Dawson, *The Government of Canada* (Toronto: University of Toronto Press, 1970), p. 326. See also Jonathan Boston, 'By-Elections in New Zealand: An Overview', *Political Science*, 32 (1980), p. 107.

[5]Quoted in Pollock, 'British By-Elections Between the Wars', p. 528.

[6]Pollock, British By-Elections Between the Wars', p. 527; see also John C. Sparks, 'British By-Elections: What Do They Prove?', *American Political Science Review*, 34 (1940), 97-104.

[7]The 1950-80 Gallup polling figures come from Norman Webb and Robert Wybrow, *The Gallup Report* (London: Sphere Books, 1981), pp. 168-83. The 1981 figures are from *idem*, *The Gallup Report*, (London: Sphere Books, 1982), p. 192. Bob Wybrow kindly made an unpublished compilation of the 1982 and 1983 figures available to me. Both these books also provide the full text of the questions measuring voting intention, approval of the government's record, prime ministerial popularity and the opposition leader's popularity. The 'additional' governing and opposition party voting intention and Conservative and Labour party leader variables are constructed simply by taking account of the identity of the party in office in the months that Gallup asked its questions. Finally, only whole numbers are used herein; the few monthly returns including a decimal value of .5 are rounded up.

[8]Each set of general election figures usually comes from the month in which the election took place. Two of them (1959 and 1979), however, were

held in the first week of their respective months so the figures from the immediately preceding month were used. The change measures are calculated from the month after the one in which the general election took place to the one in which the by-election was held. There was no refinement introduced to take account of the timing of the by-election within the month because preliminary investigation using time lags of one, two and three months before the month of the by-election indicated that the best prediction was achieved using the party standing figures in the month of the by-election. Finally, there are a few gaps in the monthly Gallup data, especially in the early 1950s. Where such gaps did not span more than three months, they were filled in with estimates calculated from the preceding and succeeding monthly figures. The only case in which such estimation was not possible is the opposition leader variable; it was only in 1959 that this question began to be asked on a regular basis.

[9]See Butler and Stokes, *Political Change in Britain*, esp. chs. 2 and 17.

[10]The interesting exception to this pattern of correlations is that between Conservative voting intention and satisfaction with the Conservative party leader. Its value is no more than 0.04, which again suggests that Conservative supporters, in being able to dissociate leader from party, are more politically aware and sophisticated in their response to party stimuli. In the broader context of constituency electorates in Conservative, as opposed to Labour, seats, this is a theme that permeates this chapter. This dissociation notwithstanding, however, the Conservative leader variable still could not be used in this chapter's analysis since it is highly intercorrelated with other party variables, particularly government approval.

[11]At least partly because of the smaller number of cases involved, the general election correlations between the voting intention and party leader variables are even higher than the by-election ones. For the Conservative party and its leader, for example, the simple correlation is 0.88, while the same figure for the Labour party is 0.91, for the governing party 0.92 and for the opposition party 0.70.

[12]The argument that class voting in Britain. especially in the middle class, is based on some notion of self-interest is the theme of David Robertson's *Class and the British Electorate* (Oxford: Blackwell, 1984), esp. Part I.

[13]The R^2 value in fact drops to 9.3 per cent. With a beta weight of -0.13 (as compared to 0.27 for partisanship and 0.22 for country), Conservative voting intention does just fail to enter the equation. As will be seen in Table 5.3, however, this variable's influence is restricted to Conservative seats, which is a second reason why it cannot be deemed important for by-election turnout generally.

[14]To substitute the party leader for voting intention variables alters neither this nor any of the other conclusions drawn from Table 5.2. Its only effect is to bring partisanship into an otherwise unchanged general election

equation. The by-election equation remains unchanged in terms of its constituent predictors.

[15]See John Curtice and Michael Steed, 'Electoral Change and the Production of Government: The Changing Operation of the Electoral System in the United Kingdom since 1955', *British Journal of Political Science*, 12 (1982), 249-98.

[16]A good discussion of how stepwise regression works can be found in Fred N. Kerlinger and Elazar J. Pedhazur, *Multiple Regression in Behavioral Research* (New York: Holt, Rinehart and Winston, 1973), pp. 290-95.

[17]It is worth noting that this same conclusion is also suggested by an examination of the relationship between turnout, Conservative popularity and its vote. In both general and by-elections, turnout and the Conservative party's vote are negatively correlated in the seats it controls (-0.26 and -0.54 respectively). Controlling for the effect of the party's standing in the polls, however, changes these figures into partial correlation coefficients of -0.41 and -0.40 respectively. That is, this control has the effect of strengthening high turnout's negative impact on the Conservative party's general election vote, which indicates that the party's being popular serves to bring Conservative voters to the polls when the political stakes are high. But when these stakes are low, as in by-elections, to control for popularity actually weakens high turnout's negative effect on the Conservative vote. By the same logic, therefore, the more popular the Conservative party is, the more its voters are likely to succumb to complacency and stay away from the polls at by-election time.

[18]Substituting the party leader variables for voting intention once again highlights the formers' relative weakness in structuring turnout patterns, especially in low-stimulus by-elections. In general elections, this substitution displaces Conservative party voting intention in the seats held by this party and it is replaced by the opposition leader and voter uncertainty variables. The substitution has no effect at all on the outcome of the regression analysis in Labour seats since Labour party voting intention itself has no effect (see Table 5.3). In by-elections, by contrast, the substitution's main effect is to make for less tidy solutions insofar as the voting intention variables are not replaced by the corresponding party leader ones. Liberal party popularity becomes the preeminent predictor in Conservative seats and it is followed by the standing of the Labour party leader. There is no change in Labour seats, which is again not surprising since the voting intention variables also had no effect in them. At least for seats held by the Conservatives, then, the party leader variables, in imposing themselves less decisively than their voting intention counterparts, leave room for other variables to assume explanatory importance. That these 'new' variables have nothing to do with the Conservative party only emphasises the potency of loyalty to this party in influencing the turnout patterns of what are presumably its own supporters.

Were this loyalty of roughly the same magnitude as satisfaction with the party leader, the non-incumbent party would enjoy a mobilisation advantage that could well endanger the Conservative party's hold on its more marginal seats.

[19]When marginality is excluded, the only significant predictor of general election turnout in opposition seats is % Conservative and its beta weight is 0.25 and the variance explained a very small 6.4 per cent. For by-elections, the significant predictors are the long-term forces of partisanship (0.21) and country (0.17) and they explain 8.0 per cent of the total variance.

[20]To substitute the party leader for voting intention variables tends to support this conclusion, albeit not wholly. On the one hand, the popularity of the opposition leader emerges as a significant predictor of general election turnout in opposition seats. But more importantly, prime ministerial popularity has absolutely no effect in either type of election in government seats, whereas the standing of the Conservative and Labour leaders are significant in both general and by-elections in them. In addition, Liberal party popularity rises to explanatory preeminence in these same seats, presumably reflecting Conservative and Labour supporters embracing of this party as an alternative to abstention or support for the other major party. Two conclusions follow from these observations. The first is that to the extent turnout levels in government seats respond to popular evaluations of the government, they do so to the party and not its leader, which emphasises the subordination of the leader to more enduring party loyalties. The second is that, assuming elections in government seats to be of a higher stimulus level than those in opposition seats, it is in their role as head of the major parties, and not of the governing or opposition parties, that party leaders influence turnout patterns when interest in the election is running high. The short-term forces that matter most for both general and by-election turnout in these seats is the standing in national public opinion of the Conservative and Labour parties. In other words, to the extent that constituency electorates even in government seats are responsive to the national popularity of the parties, their turnout patterns are fuelled more by the mobilisation of traditional party loyalties than by current assessments of the relative merits of the parties in and out of office.

[21]The full equation is % Conservative (-0.29), Partisanship (0.28), % Govt. approval (-0.25) and Country (0.23) and the R^2 value is 21.4 per cent.

[22]The means for the general election and change party standing scores are respectively: 43.4 and -1.9 per cent for Conservative voting intention; 45.9 and -3.0 per cent for Labour voting intention; 7.8 and +4.6 per cent for Liberal voting intention; 43.3 and -2.0 per cent for opposition party voting intention; 10.4 and +1.9 per cent for don't know voting intention and 47.6 and -7.9 per cent for government approval. The by-election scores can be obtained simply by adding each pair of scores.

[23]Faced with the same need to choose between the cross-sectional and change versions of a number of predictor variables in the last chapter, the opposite choice was made and by-election candidate characteristics included in preference to their change counterparts. These contrasting decisions are perfectly justifiable on good theoretical grounds and were not taken because they produced 'better' results than the other option. It stands to reason that it is the by-election candidates themselves who would be more likely to affect the rate of change of turnout than would some unlikely popular assessment of these candidates relative to their immediate predecessors. In this chapter, on the other hand, the explicit interest is the effect on the rate of change of turnout of trends in the popular standing of the parties, especially the one in government.

[24]This observation, however, does not apply to the leaders of the governing and opposition parties. When the party leader variables are used in place of the voting intention ones in Table 5.5, the formers' relative impotence becomes immediately apparent. The substitution has no effect in the equation including marginality, but when this constituency characteristic is excluded the substitution allows change in partisanship and Liberal party voting to displace the government approval and opposition voting intention variables. In other words, once again the evidence is that the party leaders variables do not tap the same strong feelings that these other indirect measures of commitment to the Conservative and Labour parties do.

[25]This argument should not be overstated. When the party leader variables are substituted for the voting intention ones, the popularity of the Conservative leader still figures in the explanation of turnout change in Conservative seats, albeit in a secondary role to the popularity of the opposition party leader.

[26]It is interesting to note that this anti-government reaction takes the form of a Liberal party effect when party leader variables are used instead of voting intention ones. The more popular this party becomes, the smaller the drop in turnout. As Table 5.7 indicates, though, its effect is subordinated to loyalty to the major parties when the voting intention variables are used.

[27]Sidney Verba and Norman H. Nie, *Participation in America: Political Democracy and Social Equality* (New York: Harper and Row, 1972), pp. 224-28.

6   Conclusion

Introduction

This book set out to examine the interplay of long- and short-term political forces in structuring constituency turnout patterns in British parliamentary elections. Its main focus has been the effect of short-term party political forces since their contribution to this aspect of the voting act has tended to be neglected in Britain and elsewhere.

Three turnout dimensions were identified, general election turnout, by-election turnout and the rate of change of turnout between these two types of election. The general hypothesis guiding the analysis has been that short-term political forces can be expected to affect each of them differently. More specifically, the influence of these forces was expected to be inversely related to the competition that they meet from other voter-mobilising influences and agencies, and should consequently have made itself felt more strongly in low-stimulus by-elections than in high-stimulus general elections. Political parties may be equally concerned to get out their vote in both types of election, but, for example, the media's coverage of single by-elections will generally be less extensive and intensive than it is of general elections where at stake is not loss or victory in one of over six hundred seats, but the exercise of governmental power for a period of up to five years. Of course, it may be that local media, which mainly take the form of newspapers, pay more or less equal attention to the two types of election, but it must be remembered that Britain's print and, more especially, electronic (radio and television) media have always been predominantly national, or at best regional, in organisation and focus. They might show a keen interest in individual by-elections as they draw near, but the attention paid to them will invariably pale beside that of a general election campaign spanning three weeks or more of intense political activity across the whole of the country.

The first point to be made is that the testing of this hypothesis brought to light a problem which complicated the process of reaching a conclusion as to whether the evidence supported or rejected it. The essence of this problem is that the categorical distinction between long- and short-term forces proved easier to maintain at a conceptual level than at an empirical one. Short-term forces were originally defined as being election-specific. A number of ostensibly short-term relationships emerged, however, that were in fact more coherently interpreted if seen as persisting over several elections. A good example is the general election effect of the candidate number variable in Chapter 3; depressing rather than increasing turnout, it was interpreted as a surrogate measure of the post-1966 growth of public disillusionment with the Conservative and Labour parties. Similarly, the constituency service variable in Chapter 2 was taken to be a measure of the organisational entropy that follows from the same candidate's successfully winning a seat in a number of successive elections. Finally, the effect of the Conservative and Labour party voting intention variables in Chapter 5 was interpreted as a testament more to the mobilising power of traditional party loyalties and less to the effect on turnout of the parties' immediate popularity with the electorate.

A good case can be made, however, for the argument that this difficulty does not invalidate the basic distinction between the two types of political force. Rather, it is a difficulty whose very presence suggests that short-term forces are more satisfactorily conceptualised as being of two types: those, like candidates' age and sex that are clearly election-specific and those, like organisational entropy, that persist over several elections despite being no less directly associated with the candidate himself. Being election-specific, the first type is easily distinguished from long-term forces, but this is less true for the second type since it differs from them only in degree and not in kind. In the particular context of this analysis, though, what does differentiate transcendent short-term forces is that their strength varies more widely than does that of long-term forces whose defining characteristic is that they are more deeply rooted in enduring features of British society. Aggregate partisanship in by-elections, for example, ranges between 12.2 and 21.0 per cent. The same figures for Conservative party voting intention are 27.0 and 55.0 per cent respectively and for Labour voting intention 25.0 and 54.0 per cent respectively. Being even more independent of class divisions in Britain, the level of satisfaction with the government is still more variable, reaching a minimum score of 18.0 per cent and a maximum one of 60.0 per cent (see Table 5.1).[1]

Granting, then, that the array of political forces initially designated as short-term can still be accepted as such, the hypothesis of their differential effect on each of the turnout dimensions can now be evaluated. The most general conclusion to be drawn in this regard is that the evidence neither wholly confirms nor wholly rejects this hypothesis. While favourable to it on balance, the support is somewhat mixed. That is, the systematic differences that do characterise the individual turnout dimensions are of degree rather than kind and this is so because of, firstly, the pervasive explanatory importance of the marginality variable and, secondly, the emergence of certain other, less powerful variables which have an effect across different types of seat regardless of turnout dimension. Both these phenomena serve to blur, but not eliminate, the distinctiveness of the short-term forces' effect on each of the turnout dimensions.

The most striking feature of the analysis undertaken in this book is the pervasive explanatory importance of the electoral marginality variable. It figures in every one of the 65 equations reported in Chapters 3, 4 and 5, and is the first-ranked predictor in 53 of them.[2] Moreover, no turnout dimension is any more impervious to its influence than any other; of the twelve occasions when it is not the most important predictor, for example, seven involve general elections and five by-elections. Precisely because it so dominates the other long- and short-term influences, in other words, the marginality variable serves to make the general election, by-election and turnout change dynamics resemble each other more closely than they would otherwise have done. To note its homogenising effect, though, is not to explain what it is about the closeness of a parliamentary contest that introduces such a degree of similarity into the various turnout dynamics. What is more, not at least to attempt such an explanation would mean that this analysis would have moved us no closer to a genuine understanding of the politics of turnout in British parliamentary elections.

The interpretation defended throughout this book is that marginality is functioning as a surrogate measure of the organisational mobilisation of the vote in the constituency; the closer the contest in the preceding general election, the harder political parties and their allies will try to get their supporters to the polls so as to influence the upcoming election outcome to their own advantage. But it is important to recognise that this interpretation of marginality's impact does *not* see it as a measure of the strength of local party organisation. As argued in the early part of Chapter 3, constituencies' marginality is just too fluid over short periods of time to sustain such an ossified interpretation of the variable's meaning; its simple correlation with itself between general and by-election, for example, is no more than 0.48. The parties themselves may even revise their definition of which seats are marginal on the basis of election results between general elections. In the period between those of 1970 and February 1974, for example, '(t)he Labour list of 179 marginals was drawn up in 1971 and modestly revised in the light of local election results in 1972 and 1973'.[3] Moreover, this institutional interpretation also carries in its wake the assumption that all parties in marginal seats are equally well organised and those in safe seats equally poorly organised, whereas Chapter 4 has indicated that, regardless of how marginal the seat, organisational entropy is more of a problem for the Labour party where it is incumbent than it is for the Conservative party in its seats.

The more flexible interpretation of marginality in terms of the organisational mobilisation of the vote does not entail this static view of the quality of party organisation in different types of seat. Its starting point is that any constituency will contain a large number of electors, usually strong partisans, who would cast their ballot even in the hypothetical situation that short-term forces, like marginality, exercised no electoral influence. The problem for political parties is not to get this type of supporter to the polls, but to mobilise the more faint-hearted of their potential voters. Their need to do this is obviously greater the more marginal the seat. The election strategies that they adopt therefore are flexible and readily tailored to this end. In particular, marginal seats are targetted in each election and disproportionate campaign resources are channelled into them in an effort to clinch victory. These resources take the form of professional agents, visits by national party leaders and, probably most importantly, the importation of campaign workers from neighbouring, safer seats. The borrowing of workers is known as 'mutual aid' and, at least in the context of the February 1974 general election, '(o)nly the Conservative parties managed to make serious efforts at (it) for the marginal seats'.[4] Aid of this type may not always be granted and some may feel it 'often more impressive on paper than in practice'.[5] Nonetheless, imperfect as its workings may be, it is probably one of the several organisational reasons why the Conservative party consistently comes across in this analysis as being better than Labour at mobilising support, and especially when it matters in general elections and marginal seats.

Granting this interpretation, it is easily understandable why marginality should be a key factor diluting the distinctiveness of the pattern of turnout determinants on each of the general election, by-election and rate of change dimensions; albeit to varying degrees, the active mobilisation of support will crucially affect all three of them. Further blurring their distinctiveness is a small number of other short-term forces that also figure in the explanation of more than one of these dimensions. The most powerful of these is MPs' constituency service in Chapter 4, which has been argued to be another facet of the organisational mobilisation of the vote in the constituency, namely the entropy that sets in the longer a seat, no matter how marginal, has been held by the same incumbent. The only other short-term forces to be similarly pervasive are parliamentary marginality in Chapter 3 and Conservative voting intention in Chapter 5.

Especially interesting about these last two variables is that they figure in Conservative and government seats, but not in Labour and opposition ones. This selectivity has been argued on a number of occasions to reflect the greater political sensitivity and responsiveness of constituency electorates in the first two groups of seats. This is not to say that they are responsive to the same stimuli. It is noticeable, for example, that general election turnout in Conservative seats is unaffected by the sitting MP's length of parliamentary service, whereas this variable is its most important predictor in government seats. Such dissimilarities, however, are less striking than the consistently similar regression outcomes in Conservative and government seats on the one hand and Labour and opposition ones on the other. It is important to recognise, though, that this pattern of similarities is not altogether fortuitous. Rather, it results in part at least from an unanticipated problem with this analysis, namely, a disproportionate overlap between seat groupings. Of the 141 government seats in this analysis, 91, or 65 per cent, of them were held by the Conservative party at the time of the by-election and the Labour party was incumbent in 68 per cent (67) of the 99 opposition seats. The overlap is not so pronounced for general elections where Labour controlled 75, or 54 per cent of government seats and the Conservatives did likewise for 61, or 62 per cent, of the 99 opposition seats.[6] Equally, though, the pattern of similarities is not so striking in this type of election. Had government and opposition seats been more evenly distributed between the major parties, in other words, the relationship between short-term forces and turnout patterns in them might have been cast in a more distinctive light, especially on the by-election and turnout change dimensions.

Fortunately, this overlap is not a problem that undermines the major task of this concluding chapter, which is to assess the evidence relating to the hypothesis of a distinctive dynamic for each of the three turnout dimensions. The focus up to this point has been on the similarity in their respective dynamics, largely because of the overwhelming importance of organisational mobilisation for the explanation of variation in constituency turnout patterns. But this similarity far from overwhelms their distinctiveness. Rather, the three turnout dimensions can still be differentiated along two axes, the first relating to the prevalence of short-term forces and the second, and more tentative, to the balance of 'national' and 'local' forces on each of them. Rather than relying on memory, the most effective way of highlighting this differentiation is to present an overall picture of the separate findings of Chapters 3, 4 and 5.

Table 6.1: Standardised coefficients for the regression of turnout on the range of long-term and short-term political forces by type of election

General election turnout				By-election turnout		
(.32)	Marginality	0.31		(.30)	Marginality	0.27
(.38)	% Conservative	0.30		(.23)	Country	0.20
(-.30)	Candidates	-0.15		(.21)	Partisanship	0.17
(.07)	Country	0.13		(.22)	Sex	0.16
	R^2=29.2			(.11)	Candidate exclusivity	0.14
				(-.21)	% Conservative	-0.13
				(-.12)	Local office	-0.12
					R^2=26.6	

Table 6.1 summarises the regression of general and by-election turnout on all the variables included in the separate analyses of the previous three chapters. The only qualification is that representing Chapter 4 are the collective candidate attributes since these seem more appropriate to an examination of the population of constituencies than are the characteristics of the individual candidates. The first thing to notice is that the table contains no surprises in the sense that the variables proving to be important in the chapter-by-chapter analyses are also the variables figuring in it. The strategy of keeping the three clusters of short-term forces separate for the purposes of detailed analysis has done nothing to distort the overall picture of the determinants of the two dimensions of constituency turnout. As would have been expected, both of them

are structured primarily by the marginality of the preceding general election, but their dynamics have little in common beyond this shared characteristic. Their diversity, however, is not such as to make it easy to evaluate the original hypothesis of a stronger role for short-term forces in low-stimulus by-elections. The problem is essentially that these forces are stronger in general elections, but there are more of them, in absolute if not proportionate terms, in by-elections. That is, short-term forces take up the top three explanatory positions in the former, with the long-term force of country a weak fourth. But this picture is reversed somewhat for by-elections where the long-term forces of country and partisanship may follow marginality in the list of dominant predictors, but these are then themselves followed by four other short-term forces - three of them relating to the group of candidates contesting the by-election and the other to the Conservative party's national standing at the time of the by-election.

There is no straightforward solution to this interpretational problem. Certainly, the importance for by-election turnout of certain of the attributes of the group of candidates on offer to the electorate, and especially their sexual mix, cannot be denied. Nor, therefore, can the impact of short-term forces in this type of election. There is nonetheless a number of reasons to conclude that, contrary to the orginal hypothesis, these forces are less influential in by-elections than in general elections. Firstly, Table 6.1 shows their impact to be more decisive in high-stimulus elections. The adoption of a less generous inclusion criterion, for example, would not affect the outcome of the general election analysis, but it would undoubtedly eliminate some of the less powerful variables affecting the level of by-election turnout. The equations' distinctiveness one from the other would, in other words, become more marked with short-term forces playing less of an explanatory role in the by-election equation. Secondly, if the characteristics of the individual Conservative and Labour candidates are used in place of the collective attributes, the general election equation remains the same. The by-election equation, in contrast, is much simplified with short-term forces barely figuring in it.[7] Finally, and relatedly, marginality and collective candidate characteristics apart, there is no evidence elsewhere in the book for a generalised short-term effect on by-election turnout. The level of turnout in general elections, on the other hand, is influenced by two or more short-term forces in each of Chapters 3, 4 and 5 (see Tables 3.3, 4.4 and 5.2).

It seems reasonable to conclude, therefore, that high-stimulus elections heighten the importance of short-term party political forces for the explanation of variation in constituency turnout levels. The intensity, excitement and anticipation surrounding general elections would seem to make the competing parties more salient reference points for electors generally and their supporters in particular. The relative quiescence of by-elections, on the other hand, seems by and large to leave constituency electorates cold and indifferent to these same party cues and signals. Although no evidence has been provided to speak to it directly, the explanation of this difference is not really that party cues are less clear in by-elections; the competing parties in fact make every effort to ensure that they are. Rather, the key difference seems to lie in the electorate's receptivity to these cues and the high stakes at play in general elections serves to sharpen this receptivity.[8]

The second axis on which general and by-elections can be differentiated is the relative contribution of national and local short-term forces to their respective turnout dynamics. Moreover, their distinctiveness in this regard is immediately apparent. To be sure, the local force of marginality is the first-ranked predictor in both equations in Table 6.1, but it is far less dominant over other short-term forces in the explanation of general election turnout. Indeed, to all intents and purposes, it enjoys the same explanatory status as the second-ranked predictor, the national standing of the Conservative party. This is then itself followed by another national force, public disillusion with the governing Conservative and Labour parties. The picture is quite different for by-elections. The local force of marginality is not only more dominant in its preeminence, but also it is followed in explanatory importance by the long-term forces of country and partisanship. It is only after these that other short-term forces come to the fore in the equation and, to the extent that these are primarily candidate attributes, they are local forces. Indeed, the only national short-term influence on by-election turnout is the popularity of the Conservative party and it ranks sixth in the list of seven significant predictors.

It would seem, then, that variation in general election turnout is to be explained primarily by national forces and in by-election turnout by local ones. Care should be taken before embracing this conclusion too uncritically, however. Again, there is no problem with the general election interpretation. But if, as has just been argued, Table 6.1 can reasonably be taken to overstate the importance of local forces for by-elections, then, by the same logic, the inflated role for these short-term forces must also overstate the local character of this type of election's turnout dynamic. It is certainly difficult not to find this argument persuasive since few other instances can be found of local forces, be they in the form of contextual characteristics or individual candidate attributes, structuring by-election turnout. Certainly, none of them does so consistently. Moreover, the sporadic examples of local effects that can be found are cancelled out by matching examples of national forces influencing the level of turnout in this type of election. The effects of parliamentary marginality and Conservative popularity in Conservative and government seats spring readily to mind. The point, then, is not that local forces are altogether without influence in the explanation of variation in by-election turnout in Britain, but that the extent and pervasiveness of their influence is easily exaggerated if assessed on the evidence presented in Table 6.1 alone.

Table 6.2: Standardised coefficients for the regression of turnout change on the range of long-term and short-term political forces[*]

	Inter-election turnout change	
(-.36)	Δ Marginality	-0.53
(-.17)	Marginality	-0.43
(-.25)	Country	-0.20
(-.21)	Δ Constituency MP	-0.17
(-.34)	Sex	-0.13
(-.17)	Δ Govt. approval	-0.11
	$R^2=41.4$	

[*] Δ denotes change

Switching attention to turnout change, Table 6.2 leaves no doubt that short-term forces are as important for the explanation of the variation on this turnout dimension as they are for general and by-election turnout. The importance of these forces is well established by now, however, and the table's more interesting feature is its indication that the turnout change dynamic is more unambiguously the 'local' counterpart of the 'national' general election dynamic than is the by-election one. In the first place, the table shows long-term forces to be less prevalent in the explanation of the change dynamic; only the country variable figures in this equation, whereas partisanship does so as well, and strongly, in the by-election one. In addition, the single best predictor is the entirely local one of how much more competitive the individual constituency becomes from the general to by-election. Relatedly, the second-best predictor is again the constituency-specific one of how close the contest was in the preceding general election and an examination of the beta weights indicates that both these variables are more dominant over the other significant predictors than is marginality in the by-election equation in Table 6.1. The only national force to affect the rate of change of turnout is changing levels of government approval and it barely manages to cross an inclusion threshold that all the other variables in the table satisfy with little difficulty.

It might be countered, of course, that the remaining constituency MP and sex variables are local candidate characteristics of the type that figure equally prominently in the explanation of by-election turnout in Table 6.1 so that there is actually little to choose between the equations in terms of their being more or less dominated by local forces. This argument has some validity; the collective candidate attributes are more powerful than other local variables like the timing of by-elections and the increase in the number of candidates in them relative to the preceding general election. What is distinctive about turnout change, though, is that the explanatory prominence of local forces would not be surprising were these collective attributes discounted in favour of those of individual party candidates. The opposite was the case with by-election turnout. Local variables other than the collective candidate attributes barely influenced it, whereas the timing of by-elections, the presence of candidates with local government experience and the increase in the number of candidates frequently crop up in the more detailed analysis of previous chapters to influence the rate of change of turnout. In short, had the collective candidate characteristics not been included in this analysis, turnout change would clearly have been more subject to influence by local forces than would have by-election turnout. And even with them included, it is hard to deny that, on the whole, local forces are more dominant in the explanation of variation in the former than the latter.

As so often previously, conclusions about similarities and differences between the various turnout dimensions have to be drawn on the basis of differences of degree between them rather than of kind. This is inevitable when working with relatively insensitive and crude data of the kind necessarily used in this analysis. Some might not agree with its interpretation of which forces are local, which are national and which of these two types of political force is the more influential in structuring which dimension of turnout. Far less debatable, though, is the conclusion that voting turnout patterns are not the product of long-term forces alone and a full understanding of them in their complexity requires that more research attention be paid to how political parties perform one of their central functions, the mobilisation of their vote at election time. Whether viewed as active support mobilising agencies, personalised in the form of the candidates they put up for election or treated as relatively passive receptors of electors' political loyalties and affections, this analysis has shown parties to play a central role in the explanation of short-term variation in turnout patterns. Moreover, varying by turnout dimension and type of seat, this role is sufficiently marked and pervasive to indicate that stasis and change in different types of parliamentary election outcome cannot be fully understood without reference to the politics of turnout. This book represents an early foray into this largely unexplored area of study; the highly speculative interpretation of most of its findings reinforces its initial observation that much more needs to be known about it if voting turnout is not to continue as the poor relation to voting choice in our overall understanding of the voting act.

Notes

[1]This line of reasoning suggests that it is more accurate to distinguish between long-, medium- and short-term political forces. At a conceptual level, this threefold division makes good sense and seems an improvement on the long- and short-term dichotomy. At an empirical level, however, its usage would only exacerbate the already difficult problem of deciding where to draw the line between the various types of political force. This is the essential reason why this analysis has been content not to go beyond the dichotomous classification despite the limitations that it has.

[2]In Chapter 5, a number of turnout change equations are reported from which the marginality variable is excluded. These are not counted in this total of 65 equations.

[3]David Butler and Dennis Kavanagh, *The British General Election of February 1974* (London: Macmillan, 1974), p. 224.

[4]Butler and Kavanagh, *The British General Election of February 1974*, p. 226.

[5]Butler and Kavanagh, *The British General Election of February 1974*, p. 226.

[6]One seat was held by the Liberal party at the time the general election was called.

[7]The actual equation that results, with beta weights, is: Marginality 0.30, Country 0.29 and Labour candidates' exclusivity 0.22. The R^2 value is 20.6.

[8]A cross-cutting factor mediating the electorate's receptivity to party cues and signals appears to be whether the seat is held by the government or opposition. This analysis has repeatedly shown that short-term forces are more influential in the former type of seat regardless of turnout dimension. This suggests that the opportunity directly to pass judgment on the government's performance increases the stimulus level of both types of parliamentary election.

Appendix: British By-Elections, 1950-1983

Constituency	By-election date	Constituency	By-election date
1950-51 Parliament		†Paddington, North	3/12/53
		†Ilford, North	3/2/54
Sheffield, Neepsend	5/4/50	†Essex, Harwich	11/2/54
Dunbartonshire, West	25/4/50	†Kingston-upon-Hull,	
Brighouse and Spenborough	4/5/50	Haltemprice	11/2/54
Leicester, North East	28/9/50	†Bournemouth, West	18/2/54
Glasgow, Scotstoun	25/10/50	†Sussex, Arundel and	
Oxford	2/11/50	Shoreham	9/3/54
†Birmingham, Handsworth	16/11/50	†Yorkshire, Harrogate	11/3/54
Bristol, South East	30/11/50	†Edinburgh, East	8/4/54
Monmouthshire, Abertillery	30/11/50	†Lanarkshire, Motherwell	14/4/54
Bristol, West	15/2/51	†Croydon, East	30/9/54
Lancashire, Ormskirk	5/4/51	†Shoreditch and Finsbury	21/10/54
Harrow, West	21/4/51	†Wakefield	21/10/54
Woolwich, East	14/6/51	†Hampshire, Aldershot	28/10/54
Lancashire, Westhoughton	21/6/51	†Aberdare	28/10/54
		†Sutton and Cheam	4/11/54
1951-55 Parliament		†Northumberland, Morpeth	4/11/54
		†Liverpool, West Derby	18/11/54
†Bournemouth East and		†Invernessshire and Ross	
Christchurch	6/2/52	and Cromarty, Inverness	21/12/54
†Southport	6/2/52	†Norfolk, South	13/1/55
Leeds, South East	7/2/52	†Kent, Orpington	20/1/55
†Dundee, East	17/7/52	†Twickenham	25/1/55
†Yorkshire, Cleveland	23/10/52	†Edinburgh, North	27/1/55
†Buckinghamshire, Wycombe	4/11/52	†Stockport, South	3/2/55
†Birmingham, Small Heath	27/11/52	†Denbighshire, Wrexham	17/3/55
†Lancashire, Farnworth	27/11/52		
†Kent, Canterbury	12/2/53	**1955-59 Parliament**	
†Kent, Isle of Thanet	12/3/53		
†Barnsley	31/3/53	Gateshead, West	7/12/55
†Stoke on Trent, North	31/3/53	Greenock	8/12/55
†Hayes and Harlington	1/4/53	†Torquay	15/12/55
*†Sunderland, South	13/5/53	†Durham, Blaydon	2/2/56
†Berkshire, Abingdon	30/6/53	Leeds, North East	9/2/56
†Birmingham, Edgbaston	2/7/53	†Herefordshire, Hereford	14/2/56
†Nottinghamshire, Broxtowe	17/9/53	†Lincolnshire, Gainsborough	14/2/56
†Crosby	12/11/53	†Somerset, Taunton	14/2/56
Lancashire, Ormskirk	12/11/53	†Walthamstow, West	1/3/56
†Holborn and St. Pancras,		†Kent, Tonbridge	7/6/56
South	19/11/53	Newport	6/7/56

†Durham, Chester-Le-Street   27/9/56
†Cheshire, City of Chester   15/11/56
†Leicestershire, Melton   19/12/56
*†Lewisham, North   14/2/57
  Wednesbury   28/2/57
*Carmarthenshire, Carmarthen   28/2/57
  Bristol, West   7/3/57
†Warwickshire, Warwick and
    Leamington   7/3/57
†Beckenham   21/3/57
†Newcastle-Upon-Tyne, North   21/3/57
†Edinburgh, South   29/5/57
†East Ham, North   30/5/57
†Hornsey   30/5/57
†Dorset, North   27/6/57
  Gloucester   12/9/57
  Ipswich   24/10/57
  Leicester, South East   28/11/57
  Liverpool, Garston   5/12/57
*†Rochdale   12/2/58
*Glasgow, Kelvingrove   13/3/58
*†Devon, Torrington   27/3/58
†Islington, North   15/5/58
†Ealing, South   12/6/58
  St. Helens   12/6/58
†Wigan   12/6/58
  Somerset, Weston-Super-Mare   12/6/58
†Argyll   12/6/58
†Lancashire, Morecambe and
    Lonsdale   6/11/58
†Sussex, Chichester   6/11/58
†Monmouthshire, Pontypool   10/11/58
  Aberdeenshire, East   20/11/58
†Shoreditch and Finsbury   27/11/58
  Southend, West   29/1/59
  Harrow, East   19/3/59
†Norfolk, South-West   25/3/59
†Kircudbrightshire and
    Wigtownshire, Galloway   9/4/59
  Yorkshire, Penistone   11/6/59
†Cumberland, Whitehaven   18/6/59

1959-64 Parliament

†Harrow, West   17/3/60
*†Brighouse and Spenborough   17/3/60
†Edinburgh, North   19/5/60
†Bolton, East   16/11/60
†Bedfordshire, Mid   16/11/60
†Devon, Tiverton   16/11/60
†Hampshire, Petersfield   16/11/60
†Shropshire, Ludlow   16/11/60
†Surrey, Carshalton   16/11/60

†Monmouthshire, Ebbw Vale   17/11/60
†Blyth   24/11/60
†Worcester   16/3/61
†Cambridgeshire   16/3/61
†Derbyshire, High Peak   16/3/61
†Essex, Colchester   16/3/61
†Birmingham, Small Heath   23/3/61
†Warrington   20/4/61
†Paisley   20/4/61
†Bristol, South East   4/5/61
†Manchester, Moss Side   7/11/61
†Fife, East   8/11/61
†Shropshire, Oswestry   8/11/61
†Glasgow, Bridgeton   16/11/61
†Lincoln   8/3/62
†Blackpool, North   13/3/62
†Middlesborough, East   14/3/62
*†Kent, Orpington   14/3/62
†Pontefract   22/3/62
†Stockton-on-Tees   5/4/62
†Derby, North   17/4/62
†Montgomeryshire   15/5/62
*†Middlesborough, West   6/6/62
†Derbyshire, West   6/6/62
†West Lothian   14/6/62
†Leicester, North East   12/7/62
*†Dorset, South   22/11/62
†Norfolk, Central   22/11/62
†Northamptonshire, South   22/11/62
†Wiltshire, Chippenham   22/11/62
*†Glasgow, Woodside   22/11/62
†Yorkshire, Colne Valley   21/3/63
†Rotheram   28/3/63
†Swansea, East   28/3/63
†Leeds, South   20/6/63
†Deptford   4/7/63
†West Bromwich   4/7/63
†Warwickshire, Stratford   15/8/63
*†Luton   7/11/63
†Kinross and Perthshire,
    West   7/11/63
†Dundee, West   21/11/63
†Suffolk, Sudbury and
    Woodbridge   5/12/63
†Manchester, Openshaw   5/12/63
†St. Marylebone   5/12/63
†Dumfriesshire   12/12/63
†Suffolk, Bury St. Edmonds   14/5/64
†Wiltshire, Devizes   14/5/64
*†Lanarkshire, Rutherglen   14/5/64
†Hampshire, Winchester   14/5/64
†Kent, Faversham   4/6/64
†Liverpool, Scotland   11/6/64

1964-66 Parliament

*†Leyton	21/1/65
†Warwickshire, Nuneaton	21/1/65
†Altrincham and Sale	4/2/65
†Sussex, East Grinstead	4/2/65
†Wiltshire, Salisbury	4/2/65
†Essex, Saffron Walden	23/3/65
*†Roxburghshire, Selkirkshire and Peebleshire	24/3/65
†Monmouthshire, Abertillery	1/4/65
†Birmingham, Hall Green	6/5/65
†Hove	22/7/65
†City of London and Westminster	4/11/65
†Erith and Crayford	11/11/65
†Kingston-Upon-Hull, North	27/1/66

1966-70 Parliament

*†Carmarthenshire, Carmarthen	14/7/66
†Warwickshire, Nuneaton	9/3/67
†Rhondda, West	9/3/67
*†Glasgow, Pollok	9/3/67
†Devon, Honiton	16/3/67
†Staffordshire, Brierley Hill	27/4/67
*†Cambridge	21/9/67
*†Walthamstow, West	21/9/67
*†Leicester, South West	2/11/67
†Manchester, Gorton	2/11/67
*†Lanarkshire, Hamilton	2/11/67
†Derbyshire, West	23/11/67
†Kensington, South	14/3/68
*†Dudley	28/3/68
†Warwickshire, Warwick and Leamington	28/3/68
*†Warwickshire, Meriden	28/3/68
*†Acton	28/3/68
*†Oldham, West	13/6/68
†Sheffield, Brightside	13/6/68
*†Nelson and Colne	27/6/68
†Glamorganshire, Caerphilly	18/7/68
†Nottinghamshire, Bassetlaw	31/10/68
†Hampshire, New Forest	7/11/68
*†Walthamstow, East	27/3/69
†Brighton, Pavilion	27/3/69
†Somerset, Weston-Super-Mare	27/3/69
†Sussex, Chichester	22/5/69
*†Birmingham, Ladywood	26/6/69
†Paddington, North	30/10/69
†Islington, North	30/10/69
†Glasgow, Gorbals	30/10/69

†Newcastle-Under-Lyme	30/10/69
*†Swindon	30/10/69
*†Wellingborough	4/12/69
†Lincolnshire, Louth	4/12/69
†Somerset, Bridgwater	12/3/70
†Ayrshire, South	19/3/70

1970-74(F) Parliament

†St. Marylebone	22/10/70
Enfield, West	19/11/70
Liverpool, Scotland	1/4/71
Sussex, Arundel and Shoreham	1/4/71
*Worcestershire, Bromsgrove	27/5/71
†Yorkshire, Goole	27/5/71
Hayes and Harlington	17/6/71
Greenwich	8/7/71
Stirling and Falkirk Burghs	16/9/71
†Lancashire, Widnes	30/9/71
Cheshire, Macclesfield	30/9/71
*†Merthyr Tydfil	13/4/72
†Kingston-Upon-Thames	4/5/72
Southwark	4/5/72
*†Rochdale	26/10/72
*Sutton and Cheam	7/12/72
Middlesex, Uxbridge	7/12/72
*Lincoln	1/3/73
†Dundee, East	1/3/73
Durham, Chester-Le-Street	1/3/73
West Bromwich	24/5/73
Lancashire, Westhoughton	24/5/73
Manchester, Exchange	27/6/73
*†Yorkshire, Ripon	26/7/73
*Isle of Ely	26/7/73
*†Northumberland, Berwick-Upon-Tweed	8/11/73
†Hove	8/11/73
Edinburgh, North	8/11/73
*Glasgow, Govan	8/11/73

1974(F)-74(O) Parliament

Newham, South	23/5/74

1974(O)-79 Parliament

*†Woolwich, West	26/6/75
†Coventry, North West	4/3/76
†Carshalton	11/3/76
†The Wirral	11/3/76
†Rotheram	24/6/76

†Thurrock   15/7/76   †Clitheroe   1/3/79
†Newcastle, Central   4/11/76   †Knutsford   1/3/79
*Walsall, North   4/11/76   *†Liverpool, Edge Hill   29/3/79
†Workington   4/11/76
†Cambridge   2/12/76   1979-83 Parliament
†City of London and
   Westminster South   24/2/77   †Manchester, Central   27/9/79
*†Birmingham, Stetchford   31/3/77   †Hertfordshire, South West   13/12/79
*†Ashfield   28/4/77   †Southend, East   13/3/80
†Grimsby   28/4/77   †Glasgow, Central   26/6/80
†Saffron Walden   7/7/77   †Warrington   16/7/81
†Birmingham, Ladywood   18/8/77   *†Croydon, North West   22/10/81
†Bournemouth, East   24/11/77   *†Crosby   26/11/81
*†Ilford, North   2/3/78   *†Glasgow, Hillhead   25/3/82
†Glasgow, Garscadden   13/4/78   †Beaconsfield   27/5/82
†Lambeth, Central   20/4/78   *†Merton, Mitcham and Morden   3/6/82
†Epsom and Ewell   27/4/78   †Coatbridge And Airdrie   24/6/82
†Wycombe   27/4/78   †Gower   16/9/82
†Hamilton   31/5/78   *†Birmingham, Northfield   28/10/82
†Manchester, Moss Side   13/7/78   †Peckham   28/10/82
†Penistone   13/7/78   †Glasgow, Queen's Park   2/12/82
†Berwick and East Lothian   26/10/78   *†Bermondsey   24/2/83
†Pontefract and Castleford   26/10/78   †Darlington   24/3/83

* Indicates that the constituency changed hands at the by-election.

† Indicates that the constituency is included in the analysis in this book.

Index

abstentionism 96
Alford, Robert R. 31
Australia 3

Balfour, Arthur 112
ballot box 25
Bournemouth 54
Butler and Stokes 32

Carmarthen 30, 54
carpet-bagging 81, 104
class 14, 35
    middle 66, 118

education 2, 3, 14, 118
    university 77
election deposit 48
electoral register 26, 45
electoral strategy 77
entropy
    natural 103
    organizational 90, 93, 94, 96, 99,
        102, 145

factionalism 93
Finer, Herman 111

gallup 113
Glasgow 50, 54
Grimsby 30, 76

hegemony
    candidate 89
    electoral 4, 24
    government 90
'honeymoon' period 43
hung parliament 9

inter-election turnout 61
interest groups 8

Lloyd George, Lady Megan 30
localism 135

Manchester 54
marginality 46–9, 51, 52, 55, 57,
    62, 64, 68, 69, 94, 96, 98, 99,
    102, 111, 116–19, 124, 125,
    127, 130, 133, 134, 144, 145,
    148, 149, 150, 151
market research 15
mass media 8

National Front 9, 54
New Zealand 76

Parliament Act of 1911 22
parliamentary democracies 76
participation 7, 8, 11
partisanship 5, 6, 62, 63, 67, 68, 94,
    97, 101, 112, 143, 150
party identification 14
party incumbency 125
party loyalty 93
Peebleshire 54
plebiscites 1
political interest 14
Privy Council 81, 90
propaganda 1
public school 77

Queen's Park 54

rational choice 2
referendum 1, 116
Representation of the People Act
    1948 24
Rhonnda 54
Rose, Richard 51
Roxburghshire 54

safe seat 47
Scotland 24, 29, 32, 35, 36, 50, 54
Second World War 22, 24
self-interest 118
Selkirkshire 54

sex variable 84, 85, 97, 98, 151
Southend 54

turnout patterns 14, 26, 33, 76, 77, 82, 111, 115, 133

United States 2, 5, 6, 7, 8, 50, 81, 136

Wales 24, 29, 35, 36, 50
Woodside 50